ROAD TRIP
AMERICA

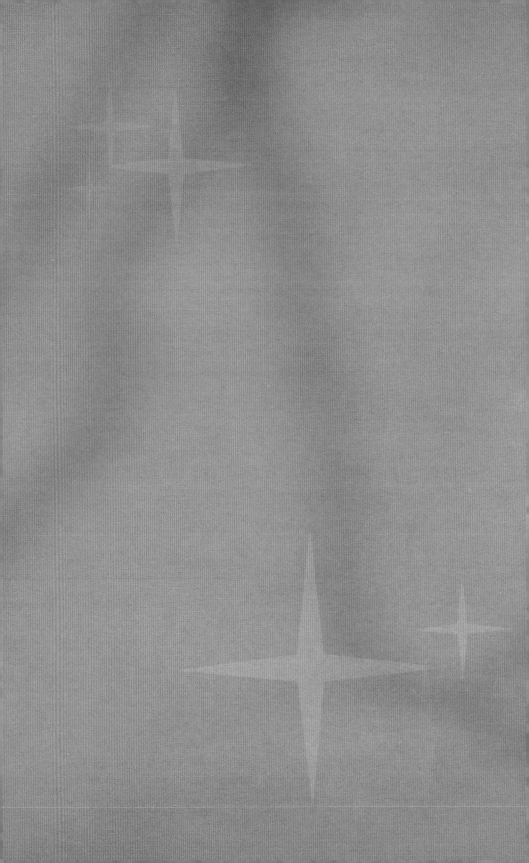

ROAD TRIP AMERICA

A STATE-BY-STATE TOUR GUIDE TO OFFBEAT DESTINATIONS

Andrew F. Wood

COLLECTORS PRESS

PORTLAND, OREGON

Design: Wade Daughtry, Collectors Press, Inc.
Editor: Aimee Stoddard

Library of Congress Cataloging-in-Publication Data
Wood, Andrew. 1968-
  Road trip America : a state-by-state tour guide to offbeat
destinations / by Andrew Wood.-- 1st American ed.
      p. cm.
Includes index.
  ISBN 1-888054-74-3
  1. United States--Tours. 2. Automobile travel--United
States--Guidebooks. I. Title.
  E158 .W896 2003
  917.304'931--dc21
Printed in China
First American edition
9 8 7 6 5 4 3 2 1

Collectors Press books are available at special discounts for bulk purchases, premiums,
and promotions. Special editions, including personalized inserts or covers, and
corporate logos, can be printed in quantity for special purposes. For further
information contact: Special Sales, Collectors Press, Inc., P.O. Box 230986, Portland
OR 97281. Toll free: 1-800-423-1848.

For a free catalog write: Collectors Press, Inc., P.O. Box 230986, Portland, OR
97281. Toll free: 1-800-423-1848 or visit our website at: www.collectorspress.com.

The journey to complete this book wound through deserts of tedium and springs of exhilaration, but it has never been lonely. I wish to thank my co-traveler through life, Jenny, and our most beloved co-navigator, daughter Vienna, for patience and good humor as we've driven thousands of miles without driving each other crazy. I also wish to thank my academic home, the Communication Studies department of San José State University, for their support of this particular obsession. Finally, I wish to thank the countless strangers along the road who offered advice, shared stories, and pointed the way over the horizon.

— Andrew F. Wood

INTRODUCTION

Past the cracked pavement of the city streets, beyond the cumbersome limits of street signs and neighborhood traffic, out beyond the edge of town, the interstate calls us on a pilgrimage. The journey invites us to return home changed, even while reaffirming the value of the place we left. The process of pilgrimage demands work and sacrifice. On the highways we make time, collect artifacts, and seek sacred places. But Americans don't take their pilgrimages so seriously that we forget how to have fun. Along the two-lane highways of the young twentieth century, Americans built thousands of individual shrines to idiosyncratic pursuits: the World's Largest Cow, a ketchup bottle shaped water tower, the Biggest Ball of Twine. Each resting spot provides an opportunity to reflect on the meaning of the American road trip, a chance to discover the soul of a nation.

The road trip has helped craft the American imagination since the days of the Model T. In the early 1900s, some tourism boosters concocted the "See America First" movement to reflect the overlapping love of travel and desire to stay home, selling the quirky slogan on billboards and magazine advertisements. Particularly in times of war, "See America First" provided a safe zone for U.S. motorists to drive, consume, and celebrate freedom. And why not? Aren't our mountains tall enough? Aren't our cities grand enough? Aren't our people friendly enough? If that wasn't enough to grab the tentative motorist, highway hucksters dotted the landscape with tourist traps — often hastily-constructed excuses to pull off the road and see something genuine. Why wolf down another fast food burger, sleep in another anonymous interstate hotel, or plunk another token in a video arcade? With a little searching you can grab a meal in a Mississippi restaurant shaped like a hoopskirt, sleep in an Arizona motor court where each room is shaped like a teepee, and play golf in an Atlantic beach-land of miniature castles. Both sorts of experience are unreal in their own ways. But, like the lyrics of a popular song, the roadside attractions featured in this volume celebrate an America that's "even better than the real thing." This book is a celebration of offbeat roadside attractions that have withstood the test of time and a commemoration of some that remain only in the form of memories and collectibles: postcards, pennants, matchbook covers, and other cheap souvenirs. Cheerfully bypassing most typical highway destinations, *Road Trip America* invites you to visit the stranger, tackier, and more personal attractions that endure despite

I've organized this book by state rather than the more typical method of crafting common themes such as architectural style or time period. That way, you can read the book in any order you choose, following the perfect roadmap of your mind. Within these pages, you'll find classic images and artifacts from the roadside of today and yesterday. This book does not attempt to catalog every bizarre, goofy, and memorable roadside monument, amusement site, motel, diner, and museum you can find with a tank of gas. Its purpose is to provide a cross section of styles, locations, and artifacts from the American highway and celebrate the visual skills employed by artists, designers, architects, and various assorted visionaries who sought to sell the glamour, adventure, and romance of the roadside. And just maybe, along the way, this book might inspire you to commence your own cross-country treasure hunt!

the growing homogenization of inter-state life. I wrote this book after seven years of road-tripping with my family, striving to rediscover the pleasures to be found off the interstate, along winding country roads, in the middle of the nation's vast deserts, and along broken pieces of pavement not even used for farm tractors anymore. My love affair with America's roadside began with the small motels that glow pink and blue and green — when the neon signs still work! However, in my travels, I discovered plenty of other offbeat attractions: blue whales along Route 66, giant Paul Bunyans along the Redwood Highway, miniature golf courses lost to the dunes of North Carolina's Outer Banks.

Using this book, you might plan out your next road trip, hitting the highway in search of kicks, adventure, and history. Keep in mind, though, the best highway memories may be found in the unexpected detours you take on a whim. Along the way, remember that many of the sites listed in this volume exist by the grit and determination of a few hardy souls who struggle to maintain them in the face of homogenizing corporate behemoths all too happy to replace original buildings and their idiosyncratic architecture with authorized museums selling today's version of company history. In all too many cases, the struggle to preserve roadside attractions has been lost, and we find ourselves left with postcard memories and faded recollections. The quirky tourist trap you read about now may cease to exist tomorrow. So when you hit the highway, take a moment to chat with the folks who keep America's road-side establishments alive. Share your stories and listen to theirs. A chance piece of advice from the person you meet at the filling station, an overheard story about a local "mystery spot" discussed by locals at the downtown barber shop, a long-forgotten motel with tiny garages adjacent to immaculately clean rooms — these are the places of which highway memories are made. So use this book like any other guide, as a starting point but not the point of your journey. While it may sound rude in any other context: Get lost — and get found at the same time.

Greetings from ALABAMA

Alabama, known as the Yellowhammer State since the Civil War, offers plenty of historical sites and family attractions, including a civil rights institute in Birmingham, the U.S. Space and Rocket Center in Huntsvlle, and the Alabama Music Hall of Fame. You can even pull off the road between Birmingham and Montgomery to gawk at a 120-foot tall peach water tower in Clanton. Plus, you can celebrate the only known monument to the Boll Weevil.

The hardy folks in Enterprise, Alabama, learned the hard way how to confront adversity. In the early twentieth century, the town's economy depended on King Cotton. Business was good and prosperity seemed assured. The pesky boll weevil had other ideas, destroying almost sixty percent of the local cotton production. Despair overcame the town. But enterprising farmers responded to the threat by switching to other crops such as peanuts. Within two years, the town's economy flourished. Remembering the hard lesson

taught by the uninvited pest, city fathers erected the boll weevil monument on Main Street. You can visit the statue depicting a woman holding a huge boll weevil above her head today, as long as the local teenagers haven't stolen it as part of a prank. It's happened before.

Tiny Town!

A monument of a different sort awaits you in Cullman, Alabama: the Ave Maria Grotto. While shoveling coal for the only Benedictine monastery in Alabama, a young monk named Joseph Zoettel dreamed of all the places he'd like to visit. To satisfy his wanderlust, Zoettel collected postcards of sacred places: Roman monuments, Palestinian holy places, medieval shrines. He also imagined visits to secular sites such as the Leaning Tower of Pisa, the Statue of Liberty, and even the power plant where he worked in younger days. He then built each structure from inexpensive stones, such as marble, glass, shells, and other random materials. Each structure conforms to the peculiar perspective created from postcards, snapshots, and other reproductions upon which Brother Joseph depended to craft his masterpieces. Set on a four-acre park, the grotto has grown to include 125 miniature monuments to the spirit and the imagination. After working on his project for four decades, Brother Joseph died in 1961, having visited only six of the magnificent structures he replicated.

In Selma, you can commemorate the events that became known as Bloody Sunday when civil rights activists, seeking passage of the Voting Rights Act, crossed the Edmund Pettus Bridge in the face of billyclub wielding cops. Visiting the National Voting Rights Museum and Institute, you can see various artifacts from the Jim Crow era including a Whites Only sign. You also view photographs of African-American political figures, ordinary folks who faced death while making their historic crossing, and a room that honors the women who often served anonymously and thanklessly during the struggle. The museum proudly notes that many of its employees and board members took part in the Bridge Crossing and are glad to share their stories with visitors.

If you're thinking of driving to **Alaska,** well, it can be done, but you're going to pass through thousands of miles of tundra, scrub, and sagebrush. You'll also see the occasional moose or caribou that generally enjoys right-of-way privileges. Riding the Alaska Highway through British Columbia and the Yukon Territory takes you past towns named after mile markers, the World's Largest Gold Pan in Burwash Landing, and not a whole bunch else. You can expect a trip of between seven and ten days from Seattle to Fairbanks (or Delta Junction, depending on the guide you follow). The road, constructed in 1942 as a wartime transportation network, drops you off into a white wilderness once known as Seward's Folly. Alaska was so named after the secretary of state who convinced President Johnson and a wary Congress to purchase the territory from Russia for about 2.5 cents per acre. Some folly! Alaska contains some of the most breathtaking scenery in the world.

Literalists may prefer the point of magnetic north located in ice floes at the top of the world, but the rest of us can visit North Pole, Alaska, about thirteen miles from Fairbanks. Here you can visit the world's largest Santa Claus, standing over forty feet tall. This jolly creature, who would terrify any elf, has stood since the 1960s and was recently joined by a fiberglass companion, another huge Santa who once entertained kids at the Seattle World's Fair.

Head southwest toward Anchorage, but stop off at Talkeetna in July to catch the world famous Moose Dropping Festival. You might imagine a nightmare scenario in which a lumbering beast is hoisted into a helicopter and dropped to the ground. Fortunately, the only things dropped are — moose droppings. Folks compete to determine the landing site of the tiny pellets and then sell shellacked droppings as necklaces and even swizzle sticks to tourists who ought to know better. The roads through Alaska bring visitors face to face

The Alaska Highway was built in World War II as a precaution against the threat of Japanese invasion. (The realization that the U.S. could move ordnance and personnel northward from the Lower 48 convinced Japanese strategists that invading the Aleutian Islands would be impractical.) Carved through 1,520 miles of snowy Yukon wilderness, the highway inspired this piece of verse: "Winding in and winding out fills my mind with serious doubt, as to whether the lout who planned this route was going to hell or coming out!"

coming newcomers, that the mayor named Patsy Ann the official greeter of Juneau, Alaska. Fifty years after her death in 1942, the town commemorated the contributions of Patsy Ann to local tourism by placing a statue of the beloved bull terrier on the spot where she loved to await the ships. As a tribute to eternal friendship between dogs and humanity, dog hairs from around the world were added to the bronze that forms the monument of Patsy Ann.

with glaciers and wildlife. But many folks choose to visit Alaska by sea. For a long time, a most enthusiastic town representative greeted people traveling via ship. In the 1930s, visitors to Juneau were welcomed by a deaf bull terrier named Patsy Ann who, despite her handicap, could sense the impending arrival of ships. Racing to the Gastineau Channel boardwalk, Patsy Ann would bark and cavort. She was so dependable at announcing the arrival of ships, and so friendly when wel-

Arizona is the land of turquoise and bolo ties, home to Cesar Chavez and Barry Goldwater — oh, and yes, Grand Canyon National Park. When you're on the road counting the saguaro cacti and watching for coyote, you'll probably follow another national treasure: Route 66. Along Route 66, you'll pass the classic Wigwam Motel in Holbrook. This architectural oddity is just one of a handful of teepee-based motels that survived the 1950s and 1960s

City Cafe and Texaco Station, Kingman, Arizona

when western themes got more mileage than today. Many of the residents are people who, as children, were denied their chance to sleep in a wigwam. Owner John Lewis represents a second generation of family members who have cared for this historical landmark. Lewis doesn't make a profit off the Wigwam, but seems to genuinely get a kick out of folks' reactions to it: "We get a lot of people who drove past 35, 40 years ago, back when their parents would drive straight through from L.A. to Oklahoma City, or Amarillo. They never

got a chance to stay in a Wigwam, so they get pretty emotional."

Drive a few miles west and you might start thinking about trinkets. What is it about road trips and souvenirs? To the French, "souvenir" refers to the act of remembering. Out on the road, hundreds (maybe thousands) of miles from home, we thrive on the feeling of freedom, the exhilaration of speed. Yet, for some strange reason, we collect mementos of objects and places in an attempt to fix them in a timeless moment where nothing moves. The folks at the Jackrabbit Trading Post understand that paradox. Since World War II, highway motorists have been drawn to the crouching rabbit that famously announced, "Here it is." Today, the Jackrabbit Trading Post offers an impressive selection of roadside gewgaws that ranges from porno playing

cards and Navajo rugs to 66 memorabilia. If you've got kids, the giant rabbit alone is worth a visit.

Of course Route 66 doesn't provide the only way across the Grand Canyon State. Interstate 10 provides plenty of sightseeing opportunities. In fact, you're bound to spy dozens of brightly painted billboards that offer traditional highway fare: cheap gas, tourist trinkets, greasy burgers — and one more thing: The Thing in Dragoon has flabbergasted folks for years with its motley collection of garage sale cast-off paintings, torture chamber displays, and a car supposedly owned by Hitler. But the heart of the mystery is simply too amazing, too unearthly, too weird to print in these pages. Or perhaps it's no big deal and hardly worth paying a buck in the middle of nowhere simply because a sunburnt billboard told you to. Either way, you won't forget your visit to The Thing.

Before riding off into the sunset, head down to Bisbee to stay an unforgettable night at the Shady Dell RV and Trailer Park, which offers so much more than a set of refurbished Crown, El Rey, and Airstream trailers. The Shady Dell is worth the visit because it gets the details right. For instance, in the 1951 thirty-three-foot Royal Mansion, you'll find a black and white TV that plays mid-century movies and television shows; cocktail glasses and an edged glass shaker; and a phonograph featuring Nat King Cole, luau tunes, and plenty of other platters to get your feet tapping. Outside, each trailer surrounds a court festooned with Christmas lights and comfy chairs. By the road, Dots Diner offers a neon-striped streamlined modern eatery with lip-smacking shakes and floats.

With a southern twang and country hospitality, **Arkansas** welcomes visitors. Crossing the Mississippi River heading west from the Great River Road, some folks make the mistake of racing across Arkansas via interstate, stopping in Little Rock perhaps, but angling straight toward Oklahoma, or shooting southwest for the Texas border. Don't make that mistake. Missing a few days in the Natural State means that you miss the chance to view multiple Popeye statues, gaze at Eureka Springs' Christ of the Ozarks, and experience the famous Booger Hollow Trading Post Double-Decker Outhouse in Dover. You'll also miss the chance to visit towns like Romance, Toad Suck, and Ink, whose moniker contains a story that illustrates Arkie humor. Old timers love to tell newcomers that Ink earned its name after a local teacher asked that folks submitting entries to name the new post office be sure to "write in ink."

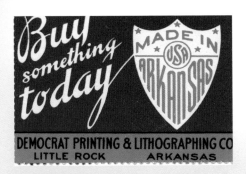

To the northwest, you'll want to stop in Bentonville to commemorate (or bemoan) the origin of a roadside mainstay that changed the face of the country. Like the first Holiday Inn in Memphis, the first Wal-Mart opened the floodgates to a deluge of interstate homogeneity, simultaneously demolishing small town economies

JORDAN'S COTTAGES - WEST MEMPHIS, ARKANSAS, ON SOUTH SIDE U. S. 70 HIGHWAY, WEST SIDE OF TOWN.

that supported Mom and Pop businesses. The visitors center, of course, recalls the heart of the empire: a humble fellow named Sam Walton who opened a five and dime in Bentonville in 1950. His original desk and pickup truck await an estimated 57,000 visitors a year who make a pilgrimage of sorts to the land of lower prices and happy face logos.

In the Midwest portion of the state, Hot Springs once boasted world-famous baths which offered nineteenth century gentry a chance to relax in almost European luxury. Today, your best Hot Springs stop lies beyond the downtown: the Arkansas

Don't be surprised when you spot a glowing white image of Jesus when entering Arkansas from the northwest. One of the Natural State's most popular and awe-inspiring tourist attractions is the sixty-seven-foot-tall "Christ of the Ozarks," a statue that was sculpted by a fellow who helped craft Mount Rushmore. Dedicated in 1966, the two million-pound icon overlooks Eureka Springs and attracts half a million visitors a year.

Alligator Farm that offers a petting zoo. You might struggle to imagine much pleasure in petting a 10-foot-long 'gator, but, fortunately, the farm is stocked with plenty of more friendly critters. Operating in Hot Springs since 1902, the farm has entertained nearly 100,000 visitors a year with llamas, goats, lambs, and ostriches living in relative ease near the namesake gators. But for lovers of the truly bizarre, the star of the show is the Merman, a supposedly mummified creature that looks suspiciously like Theodore Roosevelt.

Tiny Town!

A couple blocks away, take a gander at Tiny Town U.S.A., labeled without irony as the World's Largest Miniature City. Louise and Frank Moshinskie built Tiny Town over a sixty-year period, turning pieces of nuts, bolts, springs, miniature

lights, and various castoffs into an enchanting display of craft and heart. Originating with a western theme, Tiny Town has grown to encompass a Lilliputian amusement park, a miniscule Mount Rushmore, and bits and pieces of 1970s-and-1980s era pop culture. Look closely and you'll find a shrunken Mr. T not too far from Donny and Marie. Even with the elder Moshinskies' passing, Tiny Town continues to run as a family business, attracting gawkers who undoubtedly stop in for a lark and leave with genuine smile on their faces.

Head east toward Redfield and drop by the Mammoth Orange Cafe, which, appropriately, is shaped like an orange. To accommodate the influx of travelers responding to the citrus siren call, the owners added a cinderblock structure. Ignore that offense and focus on the sweet orange center — as good a reason to visit Arkansas as any.

For many folks, **California** emerged as a postwar dream. After World War II, returning servicemen took their families west in search of visions like the slogan of Modesto: "Water, Wealth, Contentment, and Health." Before long, many of these dreams end up in Los Angeles where you'll also discover a tiny town within the town and, nearby, the birthplace of a burger empire.

The Hollywood Entertainment Museum features a gorgeous miniature display of Golden-Age Hollywood, circa 1945, built into a stage under a thick plastic covering. At one-quarter-inch scale, the tiny town reveals landmark businesses, humble homes, and all the details you would expect from twenty-five artisans who worked five years to recreate forty-five blocks of Hollywood. The recent addition of fiber optic lighting allows you to experience the illusion of night falling over Hollywood and Vine, where the stars first came to shine.

Fast Food First – McDonalds

The search for the first McDonalds yields two museums but no original restaurant. McDonalds began when two brothers opened the Airdrome in Arcadia, California, serving hot dogs. In 1940, Dick and Mac McDonald moved their drive-in restaurant to San Bernardino and switched to barbecue. Frustrated by the hassles of car-hop service, the McDonald brothers refashioned their store around their most popular item, the hamburger, fired the waitresses, and emphasized their "Speedee Service System." In 1955, a fellow named Ray Kroc visited the bustling, family-friendly chain and dreamed up a plan to franchise McDonalds restaurants in the Midwest. Kroc opened his first McDonalds in Des Plains, Illinois. The McDonalds corporation proudly proclaims this site as the location of the first McDonalds, even though it was technically the ninth. However, the corporation also tore down this early restaurant and opened a museum where it once stood.

The Arroyo Seco Freeway, built in 1940, has been called the first freeway in the West. Built to link Los Angeles and Pasadena, the Arroyo Seco (Spanish for "dry stream") popularized the vision of limited access roads without intersections or stoplights and helped transform L.A. from a sleepy desert town to an auto-topia.

What about the San Berdoo McDonalds? Gutted. The structure built in its place served all sorts of non-burger purposes and eventually fell on hard times until a rotisserie chicken restaurateur bought the depressed property and convinced the corporate McSuits to allow an "unofficial" museum on the site.

When the road begins to beckon, head north to San Luis Obispo to visit the Madonna Inn. Thanks to Phyllis Madonna and her husband Alex, this rambling inn offers 109 different theme rooms. Depending on your budget, you can stay in the Show Boat Room, the Country Gentleman Living Room, the Romance Room, or even the Antique Car Room. If you really want to splurge, reserve the famed Caveman Room. If you can't afford to stay, you can window-shop at fancy boutiques, grab some iced tea garnished with rock candy in a copper and brass-laden diner, and visit one of the few bathrooms that may justifiably be labeled world famous. In Santa Cruz, the famed Mystery Spot continues to fascinate and frustrate visitors as it has since 1940. Apparently, Mother Nature decided that the rules of gravity and perspective needed a little goose. So here amid the redwoods, the trees bend and twist in bizarre ways while magnetic compasses go haywire. The goofy stories the tour guides have been telling for decades are worth the price of admission.

Cross the Golden Gate and journey to the Redwood Highway segment of U. S. 101, where drive-through trees point north to Oregon. Drive-through trees represent that odd convergence of autos and nature where motorists were not satisfied with merely driving by giant redwoods; they chose to drive through them. It didn't take long for enterprising hucksters to carve holes through particularly sturdy trees, allowing drivers to imagine that, yes, you really can drive anywhere in these modern times!

Even though the Centennial State joined the union in 1876, the **Colorado** territory had long provided places for outlaws and desperados to hide out. Five years earlier, lawmakers built the territorial prison, affectionately known as one of the "hell holes of the Old West," in Cañon City. Today,

seventy-seven executions later, you can visit the Cañon Museum of Colorado Prisons and marvel at its gas chamber, hanging photographs (photographs of hangings, that is), and a "self-hanging" machine. You will even learn the story of the only American convicted of crimes related to cannibalism, Alfred Packer, who avoided the hangman's noose thanks to legal technicalities following the transformation of Colorado from a territory to a state.

While heading north to Colorado Springs, stop by the World Figure Skating Museum and Hall of Fame where you can recall the glorious highs of the art form and the more recent depths to which ice skating

has sunk. Offering more insight on the Tara Lipinskis of the figure skating world than the Tonya Hardings, the museum showcases exhibits from 1946 to a present day. The museum includes tributes to skating Olympians, along with artwork celebrating those who have etched their passions into ice.

When in Denver, you'll find yourself cruising down Colfax Avenue, a twenty-six-mile stretch of commercial and architectural history. There are motels that confront the specter of drugs and prostitution by becoming paranoid encampments, bumper stickers that remind you, "America is Indian country," and the diner with the 36-foot neon cowboy and fiberglass horse on the roof. Davies' Chuck Wagon Diner has served tasty burgers to locals and visitors ever since the stainless steel box was shipped to the Rockies in 1957. Most folks will tell you that the Chuck Wagon is the only original diner shipped this far west.

From Denver you can head east or west along Interstate 70. Heading east, cruise into Genoa in search of the Wonder View Tower. You won't have much difficulty finding it. Jerry Chubbuck's Tower offers a museum of the grotesque and the unsortable. An assortment of Native murals, mutated animals, arrowheads, and, inexplicably, a ceiling covered with saws,

Once a major artery that led prospectors west in search of gold, Denver's twenty-six-mile-long
Colfax Avenue offers the longest continuous street in the United States. Driving east past classic
diners, urban towers, and tiny mom and pop motels, Colfax drivers depart the Rockies and settle into a
seemingly endless plain that stretches to the horizon.

HELLO FROM — STATE LINE TOURIST TRAP — A VERY UNUSUAL STORE — HWY. 666 - UTAH - COLO. LINE — DOVE CREEK, COLO.

SICKS MUNTHS UGO AH CUDN'T EVUN SPEL TOORIST—AN NOWE AH IZ WUN!

provide a warm-up to the main attraction: a view of six states atop an eighty-seven-step tower. In the 1930s heyday of the tower, the government certified the structure as the highest point between New York City and Denver. Once serving as a motel, a gas station, and even a Greyhound depot, the tower fell onto hard times when the interstate bypassed the old numbered highway.

If you head west on Interstate 70, keep an eagle eye open for a towering comic book hero. If you're old enough, you may recall the legendary exploits of Steve Canyon, the hero who graced funny papers during the 1940s and 1950s. The folks in Idaho Springs, a tiny mining town located near Denver, still remember. While the rest of us are stuck with rusty lunch boxes and faded comic strips, these townsfolk get to awake to a towering statue of the famed aviator. Commissioned by the comic's creator, Milt Caniff, the Steve Canyon statue commemorates Colorado service people and the adventures of fantasy flying aces everywhere.

Connecticut packs plenty of roadside attractions within its tiny borders. But the roadside heart of the Constitution State lies in the birthplace of the humble hamburger. Burgers and road trips were simply made for each other. You need only one hand to steer as you careen down the blacktop while eating your hamburger. You can get one of the nation's first, the granddaddy of them all, at Louie's Lunch in New Haven, Connecticut. Oh sure, some folks say the burger was born in Hamburg, Germany, while a zealous few

HOWARD JOHNSON'S (Winthrop Room)
929 Bank St.   New London, Conn.

point to Hamburg, New York. But drive to New Haven to visit the turn-of-the-20th-century eatery where the first burger was offered on a restaurant menu. Today, Louie's remains popular among hungry Yalies and meat patty aficionados. But be careful. When the joint is hopping, the folks who work there don't have time for kid's stuff: don't order until asked, forget about asking for French fries, and goodness help you if you ask for ketchup.

With a belly full of burger, you head north. Arriving in Hamden, you discover what must have sounded like a good idea in its day. Imagine the pitch: Let's partially bury twenty cars under asphalt in a shopping plaza parking lot to make a statement about America's auto-centric culture, and we'll call it the Ghost Parking Lot to attract misguided followers of the paranormal! It's got great potential as a tourist trap. A New York-based group called SITE (Sculpture in the Environment) managed to convince the folks of Hamden that such a statement would make a fine addition to their town in 1978. Somehow one imagines that Hamden community leaders didn't do much research on the art group's other works which include structures purposefully designed to appear as ruins. As the plaza continues to deteriorate, helped along by vandals and other philistines, the Hamden Arts Commission confronts an ironic problem that the SITE folks would have loved: How does one preserve a plaza meant to appear ruined?

Continuing toward Hartford, you won't have to look hard to find the most eye-catching car wash in the state, maybe in the country. Cromwell's Classic Auto Wash has slung soapsuds since 1986, when Anacleto Vento got out of the garment business and bought the former Pronto Car Wash. Business was successful enough,

Going at Full Speed
CRESCENT BEACH, CONN.

but Anacleto's son imagined a way to really get folks' attention. Trained as a metalworker, Vinny Vento crafted a four-foot miniature lighthouse and a windmill nearby out of junk. Wouldn't you know it, people liked the touch of originality and convinced Vinny to indulge his creative passion. Now, you'll find a menagerie of dinosaur heads, model trains, and even a statue of Clark Kent considering a transformation in the phone booth. When Christmas rolls around, Vinny clips on a microphone and greets kids through a towering Santa Claus. Classic Auto Wash has become a beloved local landmark. The Classic was even featured in a Zippy the Pinhead cartoon.

Before visiting the state capital, don't forget to stop in nearby Cheshire to visit the Barker Character Comic and Cartoon Museum, a real life Tune Town offering Pez dispensers, animation cels, and lunchboxes of every superhero you've loved but long forgotten. Best of all, touring the museum is free.

Connecting Bridge at
Langdon Islands, Norwalk, Conn.

Greetings From DELAWARE

Delaware celebrates its reputation as the First State, despite rumors that it's just a suburb of Philadelphia and that more chickens live in Delaware than people. Fact is, you'll find plenty of historical markers commemorating the tiny state's willingness to take the first step on the road to revolution. In downtown Dover, you'll find Constitution Park, featuring a twelve-foot bronze quill and four-foot cube with an etching of the document that helped shape American liberty.

Another Dover attraction may inspire you to stay longer than you planned. While an increasing number of folks spend their days in suburbia, the land of strip malls and tract houses, many of us maintain a sentimental attachment to small town life. Tucked somewhere deep in the American psyche is a dim recollection of front porch chats, evening strolls, and general stores where you could catch up with local news and maybe play a game of checkers. The Dover Museum of Small Town Life, located in a former Presbyterian Sunday school, offers a chance to relive these simpler times of the nineteenth century before the age of electricity. The museum's interior resembles a small town main street, complete with storefronts for printers, apothecaries, and even a post office.

While in Dover, you might take a break to celebrate the talking box that revolutionized the world. After years of technological innovation and legal skirmishes, the Victor Talking Machine Company popularized the use of recorded sound for pleasure with its Victrola phonographs that found their way into domestic parlors across the country. Victor also helped make famous a painting by Francis Barrauding that depicted a bull terrier named Nipper who stared quizzically into the brass horn of a talking machine that played "his master's voice."

Hello From Smyrna, Delaware — STUCKEY'S PECAN SHOPPE

AHH ....BROILED FILLET OF BOLOGNA TONIGHT.....HEH ??

While visiting the Delaware dunes, don't be surprised if you discover eleven concrete towers standing like sentries along the Atlantic shoreline. Sometimes built in as few as eight days, the towers were constructed during World War II to defend American shipping and resist the threat of invasion. Designed to last a decade, the towers continue to guard our coasts against enemies long gone.

The Johnson Victrola Museum features exhibits dedicated to the life of company founder Eldridge Reeves Johnson. You'll find a jazz-age storefront and even an original oil painting of Nipper.

Cruising south from Dover to Milford, you'll discover a regional permutation of the "muffler man," the fiberglass attention-getter found in every state in the union in the molded form of Paul Bunyan, a cowboy, an Indian, or even an astronaut. Milford boasts a giant Amish muffler man next to a used car dealership. Rumor has it that after the September 11th attacks, a patriotic soul placed an American flag in the Amish giant's hands to remind passers-by that the entire nation was bound together by our collective sadness and resolve in the wake of the terrorist attacks.

Heading out to the coast, stop by the town of Lewes where you can visit the Zwaanendael Museum to learn about the first European settlement in Delaware, called the Valley of the Swans. You can discover the gut-wrenching fate of sailors aboard the MH Brig DeBraak that sank nearby in 1798. You can tour the site that offers an historically accurate reproduction of a Holland town hall. Or, you can admit why you really came and gasp at the site of an "authentic" Merman, given to the museum by the befuddled family of a seaman who'd made his final visit to Davy Jones.

Like California, most folks heading for **Florida** reach its sandy shores to escape where they've come from. For northerners seeking relief from the gusty, snowing winters, U.S. 1 is a road of flight. Traversing the Jacksonville sprawl, you quickly find yourself squeezed between scrub and the Atlantic. You might stop for a few hours in St. Augustine to see what the fuss is about and stare heavenward in Cape Kennedy that evening but eventually, inevitably, you'll head towards Miami. Simmering land of the pink flamingo and salsa beat, Miami is a cosmopolitan bazaar of the South and Central American world. There you'll also find Miami's South Beach Art Deco district — a whimsical palate of tropical optimism given new life by the gods of hipdom.

Head west along the Tamiami Trail, carving through the Everglades. You're unlikely to see gators or pink flamingos, but you will pass through nifty towns like Ochopee, Punta Gorda, and Fruitville.

Heading north once more, stop off in St. Petersburg, formerly the city of green benches, and take a walk along the pier jetting out into Tampa Bay. The current structure, an inverted pyramid, has its charms. But squint your eyes and try to remember the "million dollar pier" that once stood here where locals would dance to jazz.

At one time, St. Petersburg was also home to the "Moses Tabernacle in the Wilderness" replica. Built in 1948, the

tabernacle recreated the site where God dwelt on earth and gave instruction. Visitors could stare awestruck at a model "finger of God" which wrote the Ten Commandments. Hungry guests had to endure the sight of twelve loaves of unleavened bread signifying the twelve tribes of Israel. History does not recall whether anyone tried a sample. Today, the tabernacle is long gone, moved up north to the Mennonite Information Center in

Kissimmee, south of Orlando, offers Florida tourists more than Walt Disney's Magic Kingdom. Nearby, you'll find an entire town built by Disney called Celebration. Designed to mimic a small southern town built in the 1930s, this experiment in "new urbanist" architecture appears to have stood for decades, even though Disney crafted Celebration in the middle of empty Florida scrub in 1994.

Lancaster, Pennsylvania. Nearby in Indian Rocks, you once could visit Tiki Gardens. Once billing itself as a "South Sea Island Paradise," Tiki Gardens featured a "Fire Mountain," floral walkways, Easter Island gods, and a host of macaws, peacocks, and other exotic creatures. Now demolished, Tiki Gardens haunts the memories of long-time Floridians who remember the guilty pleasure of rum, syrup, and dry ice.

From St. Petersburg through Hudson, a dull thud of humanity struggles along a clogged artery, snaking up the Florida gulf coast. Even now, you can marvel at stone dinosaurs, a giant teepee, and the faded mermaids of Weeki Wachee. Past the thriving Greek community of Tarpon Springs, you can imagine that you've slipped about fifteen years backward in time. You could drive back inland in search of the tiny motor courts that thrived before the coming of the interstate. Near Orlando, the Disney juggernaut craftily convinced state legislators to provide acreage and a clean slate from picky regulations to launch a kingdom of amusement and commerce that altered the tourist landscape throughout central Florida. The resulting kingdom and newly constructed planned community has inspired awe and animus in longtime Floridians.

To remember the days before Disney, it's best to drive north from Tampa back towards Jacksonville along U.S. 301. In Citra, pull into the Orange Blossom Motel. The glory days of this site are long past, but the walls still advertise "souvenirs, Florida baseball caps, Florida T-shirts, 3 for $10.00."

Georgia is a state of contrasts; it's home of the Stone Mountain Monument to Confederate heroes and the Martin Luther King National Historic Site that celebrates the civil Rights leader. Each site is within a handful of miles of an interstate that seems to pay no mind. Though Interstate 75 pushes through the length of Georgia, it has little to do with the state. Just about all you can see is the overgrown remnants of trees and hillsides as the kudzu line steadily advances. Even in Atlanta, drivers can zoom through its glistening towers and imposing domes without ever seeing the city. But if you pull off, you'll find a celebration of America's favorite soft drink and one of its most underrated presidents within miles of each other.

The World of Coca-Cola tour in downtown Atlanta drenches you with sights, sounds, and tastes of the world's favorite soft drink in a multimedia advertisement designed to convince visitors of Coke's role in the human food chain. From the Russian steppes and African hinterlands to the buzzing heart of the urban metropolis, Coke emerges as the heart of human progress, community, and celebration, or so the blizzard of ads would have you believe. Even with a museum of classic bottles, advertisements, and a soda fountain with a real "soda jerk," the pavilion saves its best for last: a "tastes of the world"

display where you can sample dozens of international soft drinks featuring flavors like apricot, pineapple, and tutti-frutti.

The Carter Museum and Library is located near the center of Atlanta and serves as the first private, non partisan venue of international negotiation. Unlike most tributes to

Carter's post-presidential humanitarianism, however, the museum tackles the challenge of convincing its visitors that the thirty-ninth president of the United States deserves more credit than he generally receives for his time in the White House. The model Oval Office is remarkable for the relatively large number of sitting and gathering spaces and the clean, efficient desk maintained by Carter, both a former peanut farmer and nuclear engineer. Nearby, a room dedicated to Carter's race for the presidency (memorable for the slogan: Jimmy Carter: Why Not the Best?) offers a video along with plenty of posters, campaign buttons, and bumper stickers. One of the best is a cartoon of Carter lead-

The segment of Highway 27 running through western Georgia, a scenic road of gracious courthouses and friendly people, is named the Martha Berry Highway. Martha Berry was a plucky educator who founded Berry College in Rome, Georgia. Among its many qualities, Berry College offers the largest college campus in the United States, covering 28,000 acres.

ing a row of trucks labeled "the South," "Blacks," "the North," and "Labor" in which he smiles, "10-4 good buddy. We got ourselves a convoy."

Drive up to north Georgia and escape the interstate traffic in search of the magic cabbage patch. "One day, a young boy named Xavier Roberts wandered into a magic cabbage patch...." From this legend, the Cabbage Patch Kids' craze began, peaking in the 1980s before being forgotten by most folks. Even so, while people who fell in love with the pinched-faced cuties moved onto the more mature obsessions like Beanie Babies and Pokemon cards, a faithful few continue to make the pilgrimage to Cleveland, Georgia, to visit "Babyland General Hospital" where Cabbage Patch kids are "born."

You can tell the blessed event is imminent when you hear, "Doctor, report to delivery. We have a Mother Cabbage in labor." Once the Mother Cabbage is dilated ten leaves (with the aid of some "imagicilla") the newborn is ready for purchase ("adoption" in Patch parlance) right there in Babyland. Georgia may be the land of peanuts, pecans, and peaches, but you'll find all sorts of crops around here.

Gary's MOTEL . . . 41 & 19 BUSINESS RT. — ATLANTA, GA.

The land of endless surf, hula dancers, luaus, and the perfect Mai Tai: for many people, **Hawaii** pretty much begins and ends with this representation. Indeed, a primal combination of postwar servicemen's South Seas memories, the introduction of Hawaii as America's fiftieth state, and *Hawaii Five-O,* a cop show based in the Aloha State, inspired a Polynesian craze that lasted through the early 1970s. Back then, otherwise staid businesspeople and suburban dwellers would toss on a plastic lei and toss back a mind-bending array of Polynesian-inspired spirits with names like the Singapore Sling, the Zombie, and (naturally) the Blue Hawaii. While few folks bothered to differentiate between the myriad geographies and cultures represented in

these tourist concoctions, most agreed that a night with the Tiki Gods provided an essential respite from the banality of modern life. Of course, Hawaii offers so much more to the tourist who seeks a taste of the exotic on American soil.

For first-timers, visiting Hawaii demands a stop in Oahu, whose Waikiki tourist strip features a seemingly endless line of towering hotels and pu-pu platters. Heading from Honolulu, Pearl Harbor's USS Arizona Memorial and Museum offers a stark reminder of the December 7th, 1941, attack that launched the United States into World War II. Turning north toward the Windward Coast, the Polynesian Cultural Center offers a simulated immersion into more than a dozen distinct cultures such as Tongan, Tahitian, Fijian, and Samoan. Heading beyond Oahu offers a surprising range of choices. Maui mixes crowded beaches with breathtaking scenery. Kauai

The island of Molokai once contained a leper colony and now offers tours of the facility.
Tourists typically arrive via a mule ride that takes them down a 1,700 foot sea cliff, featuring twenty-six switchbacks
and a breathtaking view of the Pacific. Since advances in treatment have made quarantine unnecessary, the famous Kaulapapa
Hansen's Disease Leper Colony has been transformed from a medical prison to a tourist site. Upon arrival visitors learn about the
Belgian priest, Father Damien, and the sad location from which visitors once could never leave. A few of the colony's
older residents remain at the site, and guide some tours.

promises an island of flowers, hiking, and solitude. Molokai features an active leper colony. Lanai once served solely as a pineapple plantation, though visitors have begun to search its other treasures. And Hawaii's Big Island offers a dazzling mixture of lava fields, rainforests, and gorgeous towns. Generally, a trip to the Hawaiian Islands offers the most pleasure if you try not to rush. Spending one week per island provides plenty of time to discover the Aloha Spirit. The thing roadside motorists must remember, though, is that highways in Hawaii are not like those on the mainland. While you may be used to plentiful interstates, the islands offer only three, and they're all on the island of Oahu. Otherwise, you're cruising tiny two-laners that connect main cities and circumvent the water's edge. As a result, you're going to confront a much more personal community of motorists than found on the blurred super slabs where folks pass each other with anonymous impunity. You'll experience every sort of climate, from rainforest through snow and the haze of volcanic ash. Instead of passing through these environments in quick succession, slow down and savor them. Practice patience and never use your horn unless you're offering a cheery greeting. If your blood begins to boil because the driver in front of you has chosen to travel more slowly than you prefer, and you suddenly see his hand point outward with an extended thumb and pinky, follow his advice and "hang loose." Folks who rush through Hawaii just don't get the point of the place.

Greetings FROM IDAHO

With tourist slogans like "Great Potatoes" and "Tasty Destination," the folks in **Idaho** know they have to overcompensate for visitors' limited expectations of the Gem State. Few people know that Idaho possesses the highest sand dunes in America (Bruneau), the oldest fossil (Hagerman), and the deepest gorge (Hells Canyon). You'll even discover the Pea and Lentil Capital of the World in the town of Moscow, Idaho. But in case a visit to Idaho must be completed with a spud stop, drop by Blackfoot's World Potato Expo. Built in a refurbished Oregon Short Line Railroad depot, the expo draws visitors with the world's largest potato chip, a tribute to Mr. Potato Head, a history of the 1,600-year-old Peruvian export, and best of all, "free taters for out-of-staters." That's right, paid admission gets you a loaded baked potato. Before you leave, check out the auto-graphed potato signed by former Vice President Dan Quayle, who, as history recalls, had some difficulty spelling the spud. While in the southeastern portion of

Idaho Motel Guide

A Directory of
Motel Accommodations
For Motorists

Idaho, pause a moment to consider the birthplace of television. Of course, all grand histories begin with a humble tale. In 1921, while plowing a potato field in Rigby, Idaho, a teenager named Philo T. Farnsworth marveled at the meticulous manner in which he'd created parallel rows by marching back and forth, and he got an idea. You see, Philo was a natural born inventor, the kind who'd stay up late read-ing about fantastic inventions in the dawn

Bidwell's Auto Court — On U. S. 30:N. 91 and 191 — Pocatello, Idaho

U.S. Highway 12 runs through the northern third of Idaho, roughly following the Louis and Clark expedition route. The two-lane road runs alongside several interpretive sites that provide insight into the early nineteenth century expedition that expanded the horizons of a young nation.

ing age of electricity. He was fascinated by the idea of television, a system of transmitting pictures through the air that had long been a dream of inventors and crackpots. No one could pull the trick off because of the mechanics involved. But what if a device using electrons could capture an image in parallel rows in the same manner as he plowed his potato field? He drew a sketch and shared it with his high school science teacher, Justin Tolman. You can imagine the response: "Yeah, that might work." His invention took him far from Rigby, but the city still remembers its famous inventor. Today you can visit the Farnsworth TV Pioneer Museum in tiny Rigby to thank Philo for TV dinners, reruns, and *The Bachelor.*

Head north through vast national forests and salmon-filled rivers and then upward toward the final resting-place of an impor-

tant roadside symbol. There, you'll find Interstate 90, another nondescript super slab cutting through empty plains, rolling hills, and broad stretches of the country. But at one time, you simply had to stop along the highway at the last stoplight along the massive road between Boston and Seattle. In 1991, a bypass that diverted traffic around the tiny town of Wallace put a stop to all that. But the town did not give up its stoplight without a proper ceremony. Local folks placed the venerable instrument in a coffin and "buried" it while City Councilman Mike Aldredge intoned, "Like the whippet and the buttonhook, the iceman and the lamp lighter, the livery stable and the company store, cruel progress has eliminated the need for the services of our old friend." Today, you can pay your respects to the stoplight's last home by visiting the local mining museum.

Greetings from ILLINOIS

Route 66 begins in Chicago, on a 2,200 mile southwestern descent through the heartland of America, past decayed gas stations, alongside greasy spoon cafes, and past mom and pop motels struggling to stay open. There's plenty to see, but don't be surprised when you get hungry near a town called Normal.

Fast Food First!

The first Steak N Shake attracted hungry motorists in a unique way. Imagine yourself a famished traveler stopping off in Normal, **Illinois,** for a quick bite. You find a seat at the counter of a nice enough place and marvel for a moment at the china plates placed before you. Suddenly a man wheels in a barrel of steaks, lean and well marbled. He's the owner, Gus Belt, and he begins grinding those fine pieces of meat

into hamburger for your lunch. Other folks may serve hamburgers with plenty of fixings, but this is the only restaurant chain to proudly call their meals "Steakburgers." It's no surprise Steak N Shake earned the right to its slogan: "In Sight It Must Be Right."

Down near Bloomington, stop by Funks Grove where they've made pure maple "sirup" since 1824, selling it to passers by since 1891. Why "sirup"? It turns out that adding a "y" to the name indicates the addition of sugar, and nothing as fine as Funks Grove maple needs an additional sweetening. Stay on the highway for McLean and a quick visit to the Dixie Trucker's Home. The owners of the Dixie committed themselves to staying open day and night by burying the keys to the front door in the highway. Legal problems and economic downturn forced the Beeler family to take the off ramp from their family business of three generations. But the Dixie still hangs on, serving up hot meals and maintaining a hall of fame for Route 66 truckers.

If you head farther south toward Springfield, stop off at the Cozy Dog Drive-In and sample a uniquely American delicacy. If you've ever visited a state fair or amusement park, you've come across the deep fried hot-dog-on-a-stick. Dipped in

The town of Metropolis, Illinois, prides itself as being the birthplace of Superman. You'll even find a fifteen-foot statue of the Man of Steel in "Superman Square" standing guard over his home. The town commemorates its favorite son with an annual Superman Celebration held during the first or second weekend of June. And you can guess the name of the local newspaper: The Metropolis Planet, of course.

mustard and ketchup, the meal that can be held with two fingers represents the perfect chow for motorists on the go: quick, mobile, and cheap. What's known as the corn dog began its life when Ed Waldmire, Jr. and Don Strand dreamed up the french-fried wiener stick in the 1940s. The only problem was its first name, the "Crusty Cur." Waldmire's wife, Virginia, wisely suggested "Cozy Dog" instead. Generic imitators abound, but there's only one place to sample the original. Today, the Cozy Dog Drive-In remains a family operation selling deep fried onion rings, donuts, and just about any other diet buster you can imagine.

As you head for the Missouri border, just before crossing over the Mississippi River, take a brief detour to Collinsville to see the largest bottle dedicated to that sweet and somewhat tangy condiment catsup (or is it ketchup?). You're lucky to find it too, because the World's Biggest Catsup Bottle almost didn't see the new century. Built in 1949 as a water tower, the roadside attrac-

tion advertised Brooks Old Original Catsup for decades until corporate suits decided to sell the icon. When the city ran out of money to maintain the bottle, a nationwide preservation effort took shape, selling T-shirts and sweatshirts around the world. Donations, volunteer work, and even a visit by the Oscar Meyer Wienermobile resulted in full restoration by 1995. Today, the World's Biggest Catsup Bottle attracts motorists in search of the grand and the bizarre, and those who remember when everything in America seemed big.

Land of little pink houses, small town bas-
ketball teams with hearts of gold, and field
upon field of corn and soybeans, **Indiana**
beckons the motorist seeking America's
heartland. But the Hoosier State also
celebrates one of its heroes with a special
museum unlike any other. Across the
country, you may discover hundreds of
libraries, museums, one-room schoolhous-
es, and plaques commemorating the lives
of America's presidents. But what about the
vice presidents: those dependable but
generally anonymous fellows who break
Senate ties, attend state funerals, and stand
ready in case something happens to the
commander chief?

BEAUTY PARK TOURIST CABINS   Indianapolis, Ind. Pop. 400,000
Phone Belmont 1543   Phone Belmont 0273
One and a Half Miles West of City Limits on U. S. 40
5145 West Washington St. (U. S. 40) Five Miles West from the Heart of Business Center

MODERN COTTAGES FOR TOURISTS, with Private Bath in Every Cottage
Best Innerspring Mattresses on Deluxe Springs. The Perfect Sleeper.
Plenty of Shade   Cool in Summer   Steam Heat in Winter
New Steam Heated Garages   with over head Doors
Western Union and Long Distance Service

Fortunately, a Huntington site billing itself
as "the premier learning museum of
Northwest Indiana" has dedicated itself to
educating Americans about the vice presidency throughout history, with special
attention given to Indiana's favorite son.
At the Dan Quayle Center and United
States Vice Presidential Museum, you'll

find a collection of gifts received by
Quayle, an accounting of his efforts behind
the scenes in the Gulf War, and his
attempts to bring "family values" into
political discourse. Admission is free, and,
best of all, could potentially include a visit
by Dan Quayle himself since he doesn't
seem to be that busy these days.

Tired motorists making the crowded crawl
over Indiana's roof beneath Lake Michigan
might be surprised when their stop at the
Lake County Visitors Information Center
leads to a nightmarish display of artifacts,
period clothing, and bloody dioramas dedicated to the violent life and bullet-strewn
death of John Dillinger. Wandering the
exhibits of America's first Public Enemy
Number One, you'll find the broom-han-
dle "gun" he used for a prison break and
the infamous "trousers of death" worn by
Dillinger on the night of his killing outside
a movie theater. Prior to his shooting, the
bank robber from Indiana and his gang of
outlaws left a trail of corpses during their
Depression-era crime spree. However, Joe
Pinkston, a Dillinger-phile who collected
the many artifacts found in the museum,
argued instead that Dillinger was paid by
failing banks to rob them so they could
collect insurance money. Pinkston crafted a
museum to prove his case in meticulously
typewritten documentation next to each
exhibit. After his death, the collection was

Along with its unofficial designation as the Hoosier State, Indiana is also known as the "Cross Roads of America" because of its historic location at the intersection of interstates and historic stagecoach lines. The National Road, roughly covered by U. S. Route 40, passes through Indianapolis while no less than seven interstate highways traverse the state, a national record.

sold, and its new owners ignored the conspiracy theory. Today, you may view a bloody display of the desperado's bullet-ridden corpse in wax and a simple warning that crime does not pay in Indiana.

Buckley's Restaurant
On U. S. 40, Cumberland, Indiana

Heading south past Indianapolis, you may feel cosmic spirits pulling you toward yet another freak of nature, this time in the form of Gravity Hill. Like every gravity phenomenon around the country, the Mooresville Gravity Hill sells a story of

mystery and the macabre. Supposedly a native witch doctor was buried in these parts, but his magical powers continue to emanate from the grave, manifesting themselves in the form of cars that appear to coast uphill when put in neutral. Take this tale for a spin and park your car in Mooresville. You won't stay still for long.

Before you leave the Hoosier State, don't forget to pay homage to a statue commemorating the cartoon hero of the 1940s and 1950s: Joe Palooka. Starting as an earnest teen who confronted neighborhood toughs, Joe became a prizefighter but gave up his shot at fame to enlist in the army during World War II. Hoosier-state fanciers commissioned the limestone statue and placed it in the town of Oolitic for no particular reason.

COLONIAL "MODERN" CABINS
WITH PRIVATE SHOWERS
One-Half Mile West of Richmond, Ind. on U. S. 40

GREETINGS *from* IOWA

Iowa is home to John Wayne, Glen Miller, and the future birthplace of Star Trek's James T. Kirk. Known as the Hawkeye State, Iowa was also the home of *M*A*S*H's* Radar O'Reilly. Driving through Iowa's sunny expanses, you might also contemplate the birthplace of a man who once said that all men are equal before fish. The Herbert Hoover Presidential library is located in West Branch, Iowa, on a lovely main street (Herbert Hoover Highway, naturally) lined by well-maintained Victorian buildings. Out back, walk around the restored neighborhood where Hoover lived. The house where Hoover was born is the size of a one-car garage and features two pieces of original furniture along with several reproductions. On opposite sides of the foyer hang two large quilts composed of panels of cut-out sweatshirts from schools across the country named after Hoover.

Vic's
FAMOUS FOR GOOD FOOD

Party Rooms
5601 DOUGLAS AVE.
DES MOINES, IOWA

Lovers of Robert James Wellers' novel The Bridges of Madison County can take a pilgrimage to the actual Madison County in south central Iowa near Interstate 80 to commune with the spirits of Francesca Johnson and Robert Kincaid. Once boasting nineteen covered bridges, the county features six today, each occupying space on the National Register of Historic Places.

To the southeast, if you find yourself in Burlington, seek out Snake Alley. Depending on how seriously you take these things, this is the crookedest street in the world, making San Francisco's Lombard Street look positively straight-laced by comparison. Dropping fifty-eight feet within less than the distance of a football field, the cobblestone thoroughfare was designed in the 1890s to convey horse-drawn fire trucks to danger with Victorian efficiency. The idea didn't pan out, but the street endures as the site of a yearly arts festival.

To the north, discover a field of dreams and a place the ghosts of rock and roll still haunt. "If you build it, he will come": those mystical words whispered to a middle-aged farmer struggling to make ends meet have inspired countless trips to Dyersville, Iowa. In that small town, west

of Dubuque, Phil Alden Robinson directed *Field of Dreams (1989)* a film in which ghosts instruct the film's protagonist, Ray Kinsella, to build a baseball diamond in the middle of an Iowa cornfield. The baseball field actually sits on two adjacent pieces of property, each with its own access-ways, web sites, souvenir stands, and hours. Thus, you can visit the *Field of Dreams* Movie Site which contains the house, the bleachers, and the infield diamond, or you can visit the "Left and Center" site which includes left and center field and a corn maze. Most of the activities are free; in the spirit of the film, you need only offer a donation to run the bases, relax in the bleachers, and look for the ghost of Shoeless Joe Jackson.

Slip in some old time rock and roll and head for an essential stop on a rock and roll pilgrimage. The Surf Ballroom in Clear Lake, just a bit west from Mason City, served as the last earthly site where Buddy Holly, Ritchie Valens, and the Big Bopper played. On February 3, 1959, the Day the Music Died, their chartered plane crashed, killing all aboard. Visiting the Surf, you'll find all sorts of tributes to the star-crossed trio whose deaths signaled the end of a music era, and you'll see one of the faded reminders of the big band era that is slowly disappearing with the destruction of ballrooms around the country.

Greetings from **KANSAS**

Entering the Sunflower State along U.S. Highway 54, your first stop is tiny Liberal, **Kansas.** This town manages to combine a love of L. Frank Baum's *Wizard of Oz* books with a bizarre fascination with pancakes. Liberal, you see, features the home of Dorothy, whose fantastic adventures down the Yellow Brick Road have enchanted children and adults for more than a century. The house replicates what local Oz historians believe to be the home of Dorothy's dreams. Nearby, you'll find a 5,000-square-foot exhibit of Oz memorabilia, complete with Munchkins, ruby slippers, and witches of both the good and wicked variety. And, yes, there's a Yellow Brick Road. Of course, when Shrove Tuesday (the day before Lent) arrives, Liberal assumes another identity altogether. On this day, the women of Liberal race against the women of Olney, England, to determine who can reach a local church fastest - while flipping pancakes. The cross-Atlantic rivalry goes back more than fifty years, and the stakes are high. After all, Liberal proclaims itself the "pancake hub

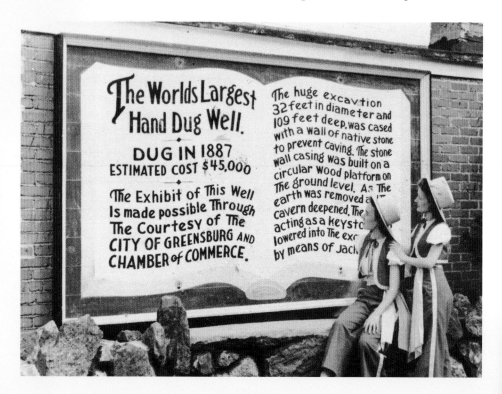

The Worlds Largest Hand Dug Well.

DUG IN 1887
ESTIMATED COST $45,000

The Exhibit of This Well Is made possible Through The Courtesy of The CITY OF GREENSBURG AND CHAMBER of COMMERCE.

The huge excavation 32 feet in diameter and 109 feet deep, was cased with a wall of native stone to prevent caving. The stone wall casing was built on a circular wood platform on The ground level. As The earth was removed a[...] cavern deepened. The[...] acting as a keysto[...] lowered into The exc[...] by means of Jack[...]

You can find a Pizza Hut alongside virtually any interstate, but the home of America's favorite pizza pie remains in Wichita. Two brothers opened the first Pizza Hut with the help of a $600 loan from their mother. They chose the humble name for the restaurant because the "hut" was the longest word after "pizza" they could fit on their sign. The original building has been relocated to the campus of Wichita State University.

of the universe." Top that, Olney!

Even if you don't care for *The Wizard of Oz* or pancakes, a trip to Kansas is better than staring at a hole in the ground, unless you plan to visit the World's Largest Hand Dug Well. Located in Greensburg, the well was dug in 1887 for railroad companies that needed a source of water for their locomotives. Measured at 109 feet deep, thirty-two feet in diameter, the well attracted locals and visitors who've tossed all sorts of strange things in for luck, including a crucifix and a rubber snake. Today, you can walk down 105 steps of stairs and get a good look at the famous hole in the ground. In nearby Mullinville, a fellow named M. T. Liggett has planted a series of totem poles that feature moving arms and legs and represent his particular views on politics and world affairs. Liggett has also painted his home in a blizzard of colors, labeling it the "Wacky Shack."

Fast Food First!

When the first White Castle restaurant opened in Wichita in 1921, their tiny burgers sold for a nickel a piece. Today, White Castle sells about 500,000,000 pieces of greasy sustenance a year cheaply enough that many folks buy 'em by the bag-full. To the uninitiated, a White Castle burger offers two and one-half inches of

square beef patty with five holes to steam-grill the onions and pickle and collect the grease that adds to its "one of a kind steamed grilled taste." Every year, the Princeton Band Club hosts a White Castle Meat Product Tolerance Marathon in which otherwise bright and healthy youngsters strive to consume more burgers in one sitting than medically advisable. At the time of writing, the Hall of Fame champion had swallowed thirty-two sliders in one evening. Fueling countless car-crazy road trips, White Castle stands supreme.

Birthplace to the cheeseburger, Post-It notes, and the feud between the Hatfields and the McCoys, **Kentucky** also serves as home to a classic automobile whose stylings have inspired love affairs and passionate rivalries. For anyone who stood in line to see Mark Hamill star in the film *Corvette Summer,* Mecca awaits in the Bluegrass State. Bowling Green offers a chance for lovers of the sleek, sexy Corvette to gather in celebration of the vehicle that guided hundreds of thousands of men through their midlife crises. The museum includes fifty models of the 'Vette (along with a half dozen concept cars), offering visitors an opportunity to view the history of the classic car in a single glance. Nearby, you can tour the factory where every Corvette made since 1981 is born.

Once you've gotten your kicks, head northwest along Highway 65 toward Cave City, home of serpentine underground wonders with names like "crystal," "onyx," and "Mammoth." Here you'll learn about

DUTCH MILL VILLAGE   GLASGOW, KENTUCKY

decades of "cave wars" in which independent operators struggled to draw patrons to their piles of stalagmites and hanging stalactites. You'll discover research efforts to safeguard and study the piles of bones left by Native American inhabitants of these parts centuries before the arrival of Europeans. And, of course, you'll find some great motels. But the best of the bunch is Wigwam Village Number 2, a collection of concrete teepees that surrounds a central playground where children cavort and adults chat.

Fast Food First!

Visiting eastern Kentucky, you'll find the birthplace of a million meals worthy of the title "finger lickin' good." It all began here with a broke fellow named Harland Sanders. He'd been a correspondence school-trained lawyer, a steamboat ferry operator, and an insurance salesman, but Sanders' greatest skill was pressure-cooking chicken. During the Depression, Sanders perfected the use of "eleven herbs and spices" while operating a small gas station, motel, and cafe in Corbin, Kentucky.

Did you know. . .

If you're heading for Louisville, drop by Kaelin's Restaurant to celebrate the site of the world's first cheeseburger, if you believe their story. As you'd guess, several other locations - most notably Pasadena and Denver – lay claim to that honor as well. But Kaelin's offers proof in the form of a 1934 menu that advertises the delicacy for fifteen cents. Stop by and taste for yourself, and as their slogan goes "if you can't stop, please wave."

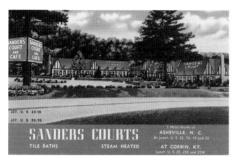

Business was good, and Harland's reputation grew so fast that the governor made Harland an honorary Kentucky Colonel for his culinary contributions. However, when Interstate 75 was constructed, bypassing Corbin, Colonel Sanders was forced to sell his business and (legend has it) rely on Social Security checks to make ends meet. But instead of sitting home, Harland hit the road. With a handshake deal for anyone who'd try his secret recipe, Harland set out to earn a nickel for each bird the new Kentucky Fried Chicken could sell. Selling the business, Harland served as the corporate pitchman until his death at ninety years of age. Today, you can visit a refurbished Sanders Cafe in Corbin and tour a museum and advertising exhibit dedicated to the history of Kentucky Fried Chicken and the honorary colonel who emerged as a hero of the fast food wars.

Before leaving Kentucky, head to Louisville and celebrate an essential part of America's Pastime. Just imagine the crack of the bat sending a tightly wound sphere into the stands. The crowd erupts and baseball history continues into the new century. Plenty of tall tales surround the great game of baseball, and a plenty tall bat commemorates its significance to pop culture. Visit the Louisville Slugger Museum and gape at the seven-story, 68,000-pound colossus sitting at just the perfect angle to be picked up by the baseball gods for a quick inning or two. Inside, you'll find a twenty-one-ton salute to baseball illustrated by a huge glove made from Kentucky limestone.

Your primary image of **Louisiana** might be of New Orleans' French Quarter, where manic revelry has caused more hangovers per square mile than any other location in America. However, you can also experience the Old South architecture of the plantation region through which the Great River Road makes its descent toward the Gulf of Mexico. Or you can head west toward Cajun country, where bounteous bayous and zydeco music create a zesty combination. Lovers of good fishing might head further north to the land of king mackerel, speckled trout, and wahoo fish. In other words, there are plenty more kicks to be found in the Pelican State than waiting for tipsy college students to disrobe in exchange for plastic beads on Mardi Gras.

Your first stop for the odd and offbeat ought to be the UCM (pronounced You See 'Em), whose initials stand for Unusual Collections and Miniature Town. It's in Abita Springs, near New Orleans. An "eclectic collection" serves merely to understate a truly bizarre mena-gerie that includes a stuffed twenty-two-foot "bassi-gator" and an equally disturbing "dogiga-tor," watching over a collection of rusting barbed wire. Visiting this converted gas station that has become the obsession of local artist John Preble, you'll also find a Mardi Gras diorama constructed of recyclable material, along with "found art" and

an Airstream trailer sporting a UFO that crashed into its side one night. Graphic arts aficionados will appreciate the gallery of "paint by numbers" masterpieces and the collection of pulp fiction covers. Perhaps the neatest exhibit is Preble's "House of Shards," a cottage covered with thousands of pieces of junk turned into art.

New Orleans also features Storyland, a Mother Goose-style park that offers storybook-based rides for lovers of Peter Pan, Old King Cole, and Little Red Riding Hood. For folks interested in a decidedly more exotic theme, the French Quarter-based Voodoo Museum seeks to educate its visitors about the history and powers of the mystical faith whose adherents seek to tap into a river of spiritual power that flows through us all. While it's best to visit the place and see for yourself, the museum's website allows you to send "spell mail" incantations to friends or foes whom you wish to influence. Want to keep your man from cheating? Make an enemy flee?

Court of Two Sisters

THE NATION'S MOST ATMOSPHERIC DINING ROOM
613 RUE ROYAL 614 RUE BOURBON
VIEUX CARRE NOUVELLE ORLEANS

imagination, most probably because of their bloody deaths at the hands of law officers on a lonely stretch of road near Gibsland, Louisiana. Today, you can venture to the site where their stolen car was riddled with 167 bullets and take a photograph of the marker commemorating their gory demise: "On this site May 23, 1934, Clyde Barrow and Bonnie Parker were killed by Law Enforcement Officers." Or, better yet, you can visit Gibsland during the weekend nearest that date each year for the town's "Authentic Bonnie & Clyde Festival." Yes, actors and locals dress up in 1930s fashion and shoot it out through the streets of Gibsland. Though it's usually kept at another, unspecified location, during this weekend celebration you can also see the "death car" from the 1967 film that glamorized the fast life and violent death of the two star-crossed desperados.

Control a prosecuting attorney? The voodoo museum offers a cure.

For some folks, the best reason to visit Louisiana may be found in the legacy of two shot-up bank robbers who got great press coverage. Who can explain America's obsession with Bonnie and Clyde? The Depression-era bank robbers went on a multi-state crime spree, and their miraculous escapes from tourist court ambushes and highway stops captured the national

PRETTY ACRES MOTEL *and Country Club*

NEAR COVINGTON, LOUISIANA U.S. Hwy. 190

phones 471 465

Perhaps the second most basic theme of road travel postcards — besides "wish you were here" — was "thank goodness you're home." Highway travel was not nearly as glamorous as the travel books said. Moreover, most tourist lodgings were little more than shacks thrown up next to a gasoline pump. Maybe you could buy some homemade sandwiches from the owner or go into town for fried chicken and an orange soda, but you almost always provided your own linens and were lucky if your cabin wasn't a glorified outhouse. Consider the Underwood Motor Camp, once located in Portland, **Maine.** Haphazard cabins and dirt roads attracted early motorists seeking to get away from it all. Today, lodgings in the Pine Tree State offer more comfort, while the roadside attractions offer a more global appeal.

Tiny World!

For example, instead of journeying out of state in search of one of the nation's "tiny towns," you can enjoy the grand spectacle of a tiny world! Drive to Yarmouth and look through the three-story atrium of the DeLorme mapmakers. There you can gaze upon the forty-one-foot-diameter, 6,000-pound "Eartha" globe spinning on a realistic axis. Take the tour and discover the detail to be found on the world's largest globe. Eartha is covered with a miniature scale (1 inch = 16 miles) of oceans, highways, and other forms of natural and human development. The computer-generated image represents enough information to fill about 214 CD-ROMs. Another way to experience the smallness of our blue planet is to journey to Lynchville, Maine, in search of their famous road sign. Suddenly you're fourteen miles from Norway, fifteen miles from Paris, thirty-seven miles from Mexico, and merely ninety-four miles from China. Yes, these burgs all lie in the vicinity of Lynchville.

Bay and Camping Field, Underwood Motor Camp, R. F. D. No. 4, Portland, Me.

If your journey takes you to Lisbon Falls and you find yourself a bit thirsty, goodness help you if you ask for a typical soda at a fast food restaurant. This is Moxie country. While initially sold as a patent medicine for various nervous disorders, including "softening of the brain," the New England-based beverage quickly adapted itself as a soft drink. Moxie burrowed itself into the public consciousness with the aid of a seemingly ubiquitous "Moxie Man," whose vigorous appearance,

Did you know. . .

Heading east? Why not stop at the town of Eastport, the easternmost point of the United States? A small town of about 2,000 folks living on Moose Island, Eastport boasts unspoiled beaches, tidal covers, and inland lakes. But the most memorable part of your visit comes in the morning: Eastport claims to get the first rays of sun in the country.

piercing stare, and outstretched index finger practically dared a passersby to drink or fight. Made from gentian-root extract, Moxie offers a taste closer to cough syrup than creme soda and was largely abandoned upon the arrival of sweeter soft drinks. But true Moxie-lovers never gave up; they formed a Moxie Militia, a New England Moxie Congress, and they even celebrate an annual Moxie Days Festival in Lisbon Falls, in which 15,000 spunky Moxie lovers gather each July to tell stories, trade memorabilia, and remind the unbelievers to "Make Mine Moxie."

10. SUNSET AT CAMP
Androscoggin County

Properly fortified, head north to Bangor in search of the "real" home of mythical outdoorsman Paul Bunyan. Sure, some folks say the lumberman who carved the Grand Canyon and formed lakes with his footsteps was born in Minnesota. But Bangor historians proudly trace the lineage of Paul and his companion, Babe the Blue Ox, to Maine backwoods lumberjacks. To strengthen their claim, Bangor is home to a thirty-one-foot-high bearded statue whose very presence proclaims to all the world that Maine is home to Paul Bunyan.

Many states have been called upon to sacrifice blood and treasure for the greater good, but **Maryland** gave up land to help form the District of Columbia, the capital of the United States. Visiting the district, you cannot help but feel overwhelmed at the sight of monuments large and small. Standing in line to visit the White House, listening to the tale of Lincoln's assassination in Ford's Theatre, cracking wise about seeing shadows in the Watergate complex: these are essential components of the D.C. road trip. But don't forget that Maryland offers plenty to explore as well.

Visitors to Baltimore's Great Blacks in Wax Museum discover more than a pithy name. They encounter over 100 life-sized reproductions of great persons of African descent in various historical settings. The museum aims to educate and uplift young people while reminding their elders of the dangers of racism. Set within a converted fire station, the museum offers figures ranging from Egyptian Imhotep and

Russian poet Pushkin to more recent civil rights leaders and space pioneers. The museum also features a model slave ship where viewers can get a hands-on, up-close look at a harrowing part of history. With the aid of fundraisers and matching grants,

Great Blacks in Wax has transformed itself from a tiny 1,200-square-foot space to its current location of more than 30,000 square feet — and plans to continue growing to celebrate the contributions of African-Americans throughout history.

While driving through the Maryland panhandle, don't be surprised when you spy a billboard that advertises, "Noah's Ark Being Rebuilt Here." Since 1974, the Frostburg Ark has risen slowly alongside Interstate 68 as a beacon of God's love and a warning about the imminent return of Jesus. The ark first emerged in a vision implanted within the God-fearing brain of

Richard Greene, who imagined the biblical structure located on a hillside. With his wife, Lottie, Richard has collected donations to construct "God's Ark of Safety." Planned according to original specifications — 450 feet long, 75 feet wide, and 45 feet high — the Frostburg Ark exists as a matrix of red girders. But God continues to provide and the promise unfolds year by year. When will the ark be completed? God works in mysterious ways, so no one has a clue. The Greenes emphasize that the ark is not designed to forecast another global deluge, but you might want to pack an umbrella anyway.

Heading for Havre de Grace, near the northeast corner of Maryland, you'll spot another of the hundreds of "muffler men" placed in apparently strategic locations around the country. Whether they have some cosmic purpose or nefarious scheme in their fiberglass minds remains a mystery. But this one makes its military purpose clear. Dressed in chocolate chip fatigues, the Desert Storm Muffler Man guards Lynch's Super Service as it has since 1991 when Ron Lynch painted the twenty-foot high statue to support the troops serving America overseas.

THE WASHINGTON MAYFLOWER RESTAURANT

2B-H66

Massachusetts is home to the nation's first subway system, inspiration for the Fig Newton, and birthplace of the birth control pill. If your journey takes you to Rockport, you'll also pass by a house made mostly of newspaper. From the 1920s through the 1940s, Elis Stenman built his house out of paper, a thrifty means of insulation. Of course, once he got started, newspaper furniture seemed like an appropriate next step. Today, the Paper House is a museum to Stenman's peculiar vision that includes a desk made entirely from the Christian Science Monitor. Perhaps he was inspired by a Mapparium located in the Christian Science Publishing Society building to the south in Boston. Often called the "globe room," the Mapparium takes you inside a three-dimensional map of the world, roughly thirty feet in diameter, composed of 608 stained-glass panels. Representing 1935 borders, the Mapparium offers a charming experience of time travel.

Fast Food First!

In nearby Quincy you'll struggle to recall an important Massachusetts export: Howard Johnson's. Once known for more than interchangeable mid-priced hotels, HoJo was one of the nation's first franchise ice cream parlors and restaurants that rose in the 1930s, collapsed in the war years, reemerged in the 1950s and is all but dead today. The famous orange roof, the Simple Simon and Pie Man logo, the twenty-eight flavors, the "frankforts" and clam strips have suddenly passed into memory, with only a handful of Howard Johnson's eateries in operation. It began when Howard Johnson bought a corner drugstore in Quincy, Massachusetts, and discovered he could reap profits by doubling the butterfat in the ice cream he sold. Fairly soon he brought the same caloric cleverness to his

hot dogs, cooking them in a butter sauce. Occupying prime real estate on newly created turnpikes, Howard Johnson's grew in the 1930s. World War II driving restrictions forced the closure of most of these roadside restaurants within about five years. However, the franchised name of "Howard Johnson" resonated with freeway folk, so much so that Howard Johnson reenergized his restaurant business and entered the motor lodge business. By 1975,

Did you know. . .

Labeling itself as "the largest, most complex and technologically challenging highway project in American history," Boston's Big Dig seeks to place much of the city's interstate highways underground or underwater and repair the damage done by 1960s-era "urban renewal" projects. The estimated cost of the fifteen-year project is $15 billion.

the company (then led by Johnson's son) expanded the restaurant empire to 1,000 locations. However, a series of corporate turnovers and questionable brand changes resulted in the near-death of Howard Johnson's restaurants and ice cream shops. Unable to compete with burger chains, almost every Howard Johnson's was sold off or shuttered; only about a dozen remain.

You will find far more to memorialize one of Massachusetts's favorite sons. The John F. Kennedy Library and Museum offers a rich and engaging experience. Located in Boston, the library is likely the most powerful of the major presidential sites. Every section offers videos, music, documents, and other mementos of Kennedy's life, presidency, assassination, and legacy. Walk through recreations of the campaign trail and view a television-studio perspective on the Kennedy-Nixon debate. Even now, it's hard to stifle a laugh when the junior senator from Massachusetts lambastes the vice president for a litany of sins. Given a chance to respond, the hapless Nixon wipes off a gallon of sweat before muttering that he has no response. With a long memory and a still-vibrant family legacy, the Kennedy name continues to be synonymous with Massachusetts.

Michigan features dozens of pop culture meccas: the Amway headquarters in Ada, a giant reproduction of Joe Louis' fist in Detroit, and one of the truly great presidential museums. The Gerald Ford Museum in Grand Rapids focuses on an oft-neglected part of American history, a time in which a president confronted post-Watergate cynicism, two assassination attempts, and an American merchant ship off the coast of Cambodia was captured; the rise of disco is even discussed. Filled with multimedia exhibits, the museum offers visitors a chance to deliver a presidential address with the aid of a tele-prompter, study the outspoken life of Betty Ford, and reacquaint yourself with a time most folks would rather forget.

While motoring through the Great Lakes State, head southeast on the "road to Wellville." Visiting Battle Creek, you can walk the very ground where Dr. John Harvey Kellogg dreamed up his brand of cereal that would reinvent how America ate breakfast. In the mid-nineteenth century, Kellogg directed a sanitarium where members of the Seventh-Day Adventist Church sought to purify their bodies while perfecting their spiritual lives. Problem was, their strict diets made for bland meals. So, Kellogg experimented with various grains and invented the flake cereal now immortalized in Cereal City, USA. A slightly sugared celebration of the Kellogg company's history and impact, Cereal City features cobble-stoned streets, a simulated production line, and plenty of classic advertisements in all sorts of media which immerse you in the history of a health fad that became an institution.

From food to foolery, Michigan reminds you how folks love to be tricked. P.T. Barnum knew it and so does Marvin Yagoda. Full of mischief and humbug, Marvin's Marvelous Mechanical Museum in Farmington Hills offers an amazing collection of vintage coin-op machines, magician posters, video games, and historical oddities. Bring your quarters for cheap thrills. See the mysterious two-headed baby! Test your nerve against a mechanical barking dog! Wonder at the predictions of the robotic grandmother who tells your future! You'll also discover a replica electric chair just like the one that fried thirty people in Sing Sing. You'll also learn about one of the great practical jokes of the nine-

THE ELMS MOTEL
South Dort Highway on U. S. 10, Flint, Michigan

Did you know. . .

The Michigan town of Novi supposedly gets its name from its location near a stagecoach. Local wags will tell you that the numbered stop No. VI, in Roman numerals, was shortened to NoVI - or Novi. No one is quite sure whether the story is accurate, but few folks care to imagine another story as clever as that one.

teenth century, involving the Cardiff giant. Turns out an atheist thought he'd pull a prank on local fundamentalists who believed literally in the existence of prehistoric giants who roamed the earth according to scripture. The atheist arranged for a fake statue to be dug up on his farm and sold tickets to gawkers for fifty cents a gander. When folks figured out the deception, the resulting brouhaha inspired the phrase, "There's a sucker born every minute" (as well as a charming *Simpsons* episode, lovers of the animated show might recall). Either way, you can see the "real" fake giant at Marvin's Marvelous Mechanical Museum.

"LAKE BREEZE CABIN COURT" — St. Joseph, Michigan

Heading south from Michigan, turn-of-the-century motorists could take the Dixie Highway, a north-south route stretching from the Great Lake State to the Sunshine State. In fact, the Michigan terminus represented the highway's East line — a corridor passing from Sault Sainte Marie through Chicago, Toledo, Lexington, Savannah, and Jacksonville before culminating in Miami Beach. Along the way, some of the first modern roadside amusements and rest stops of the twentieth century were built. With the arrival of the numbered highway system, and the eventual emergence of the interstates, the Dixie (like most of the pre-1925 named trails) lost itself to history, only to be discovered occasionally in small town main streets, faded postcards, and memories.

Greetings from MINNESOTA

LAND OF 10,000 LAKES

It's been a while since America made the most steel, the most television sets, and raised the most hogs. But we still have the largest Jolly Green Giant statue you'll ever find in Blue Earth, **Minnesota.** Surely you have more choices than Brainerd to see Babe the Blue Ox. Maybe if you hunt long enough, you'll discover some long- forgotten ear-of-corn water tower to rival that found in Rochester. And you aren't stuck with Darwin if you must visit the World's Largest Ball of Twine. You'll find competitors for that honor at Cawker City, Kansas, and Branson, Missouri. But only one state is bold enough to bring these monstrous giants together. Since the 1960s, the folks at the Minnesota Historical Society have

CAFETERIA

FOODS PREPARED TO INVITE YOUR SELECTION

documented a growing collection of huge people, animals, and objects throughout the Land of 10,000 Lakes. So strap on your snow chains, check the antifreeze, and head north to the land where giant lawn chairs, trolls, and snowmen cavort in harmony. Pop satirist "Weird Al" Yankovic memorialized one of these treasures with his tune "The Biggest Ball of Twine in Minnesota." Celebrating the accomplishment of Darwin's Francis A. Johnson, the tune tells the story of a family who had already pretty much seen it all:

"Like Elvis-a-Rama, the Tupperware Museum, The Boll Weevil Monument, and Cranberry World, The Shuffleboard Hall of Fame, Poodle Dog Rock, and the Mecca of Albino Squirrels."

But the biggest, best, and wildest adventure awaited as they drove for "three whole days and nights" to catch a glimpse of one man's obsession with twine. Today, the 8.7-ton, forty-foot round ball struggles with more recent competitors as the world's largest. Folks in Cawker City claim their ball is the biggest twine-sphere created by one man. Since then, other upstarts have entered the game, each offering a unique form of measurement to prove that their twine-ball should be crowned king. Sadly, the creator Mr. Johnson stopped spinning his web in 1989. A writer for Minnesota

WORLD'S LARGEST MUSKIE DRIVE-IN
Located 3 miles west of Bena, Minn., on U. S. Highway No. 2
65 feet long and 14 feet wide, with a 16 foot high tail
Root Beer, Hamburgers, Hot Dogs served inside
Wayne and Lil Kumpula, Props.

Public Radio offers a sad epitaph for the life of the Midwestern spinner, noting that some family members fear his death by emphysema resulted from his years of inhaling twine fibers. No wonder Darwin folks placed their town's greatest attraction within a Plexiglas pagoda.

Before you leave Minnesota, you ought to pay homage to the place that launched a thousand bus trips; Hibbing is the home

of the American bus industry. The Greyhound Bus Origin Museum celebrates bus terminals which represent the democratic potential of American mobility. In towns large and small, the interstate bus promised a one-way ticket for anyone overcome by wanderlust. Bus depots also offered a greasy spoon for late night burger cravings, a chance to pick up a magazine, and long benches for late night slumber. Soldiers heading for war, families heading for a new life, loners just passing through — pretty much everyone a generation ago spent some time in a bus terminal. Greyhound started running buses in 1914 when Carl Eric Wickman charged fifteen cents for miners who needed a lift between Hibbing and Alice, Minnesota. Today, you can visit the museum to see half a dozen historical buses, including a 1914 Hupmobile, a 1936 Super Coach, and even a 1956 Scenicruiser with an extended roof that offered motorists a mobile panorama of the American countryside.

A roving gambler sets his sights on glory but needs a home to hatch his plan. A kid comes to a crossroad and bargains with the devil. A fellow decides to bottle some brain and nerve tonic that also happens to taste pretty good. Feeding the fertile imagination of Bob Dylan, inspiring the legend of the delta blues, and launching a soft drink empire as the site of the first Coca-Cola bottler, Highway 61 is a road of dreams. Caressing **Mississippi's** western border through towns such as Tunica, Greenville, Vicksburg, and Natchez, 61 shares the wandering path of the Great River Road continuing its national trace toward the Gulf of Mexico.

Symbolically, you might start just north of the state border on Beale Street in Memphis, where ancient and wannabe blues musicians infuse the aroma of barbecue and the sweat of beer glasses with laments of pain and notes of redemption. Heading south, you'll stop in Clarksville at

the junction of Highways 61 and 49, the crossroad where Robert Johnson supposedly sold his soul to the devil in return for his near-miraculous musical talent. Near the mythical site, the Delta Blues Museum operates out of a refurbished train depot. Celebrating the music of Ma Rainey, Muddy Waters, John Lee Hooker, and others who form a musical chain of sorrows, the museum provides a fine introduction to a uniquely American synthesis of styles and histories.

Heading south, you'll amble through Greenville, which proclaims itself the Heart and Soul of the Delta. Pause a while and imagine water covering the spot where you stand. In 1927, the Mississippi overflowed its banks and blew out its levees from Illinois southward, causing a watery rampage that inundated towns and villages along the shore. A small museum in Greenville commemorates the tragedy while reminding its visitors of the price

paid in frayed race relations when relief efforts in the flood aftermath concentrated on the city's white population, leaving black sharecroppers to suffer. Contributing to a northward migration of southern blacks, the flood reshaped the cultural landscape as much as it altered the physical one.

Heading further along Highway 61, the heat coming up from the road becomes oppressive. It's time for a break and maybe something cold to drink. While Civil War buffs will marvel at the history emanating from the site where General Grant maintained his forty-seven-day siege, don't forget to stop at the Biedenharn Coca-Cola Museum in downtown Vicksburg. Featuring an 1890-era candy store, advertising displays, and a reproduction bottling plant, the museum may not be as flashy as the corporate behemoth version in Atlanta, but Vicksburg proudly remains the first place where the sugary soft drink was bottled. Winding up in Natchez for the

evening, stop by a site that epitomizes the lengths to which American roadside architecture reminds us of our past, both good and bad. Mammy's Cupboard, standing twenty-eight feet tall, is a restaurant where you eat in the hoopskirt of a black woman. Heading north through the coastal pines and hills region, stop off briefly in the town of Tupelo where Elvis Presley was baptized in the waters of the cultural reservoir of blues and country. The shotgun shack where the King of Rock and Roll was born stands today in humble contrast to the extravagance of Graceland to the northwest.

Whenever your Route 66 journey takes you through St. Louis, **Missouri,** it's always a good idea to stop at Ted Drewes Frozen Custard. Even in midweek, the size and enthusiasm of the crowd often mirrors that of a Hollywood movie premiere. Some locals come in shorts and T-shirts, while some of the women wait in dresses and heels. Inside the building, about twenty yellow-shirted teenagers hustle under the crush of business as cars stream in and out of the parking lot. Ted Drewes Frozen Custard has been here since 1929 and used to be about a third of its current size. For years, the owners petitioned the city for permission to enlarge the building so that the hundreds of locals and out-of-towners wouldn't have to wait so long in line for a taste of concrete, that famous vanilla-flavored custard named for its amazingly thick texture. Today Ted Drewes booms alongside the Mother Road. Grab something cold and hit the road south.

Along your way, you might notice a bumper sticker that reads "Your Place, My

Place — or — Coral Courts." The bumper sticker is in reference to the most famous "hot pillow" joint ever built. The Coral Court Motel, located on the outskirts of St. Louis, featured garages that led directly into the bungalow-style rooms — permitting anonymous entrance for amorous drivers seeking to avoid public scrutiny. Architecturally, the motel offered a stunning example of streamlined moderne style with its block glass and ninety-degree curves. If ever there was a motel that appeared to be built in a windtunnel, this was it. Sadly, the Coral Court fell into disrepair when its original owners could no longer maintain the famed motel. Despite the best efforts of an ad hoc preservation society, the Coral Court was demolished in 1995 to make way for a housing complex. Fortunately, through the boosterism of folks like photographer Shellee Graham, whose photos and recent book on the motel stoked memories of passionate encounters in the famed "no tell motel," one bungalow was dismantled and rebuilt in the Museum of Transportation in St. Louis. With this semi-permanent exhibit, folks can still wistfully recall special moments in a motel whose rooms were available "for varying lengths of stay."

Cruising over the undulating hills and through the quaint towns of Missouri, it's no wonder American and European film-

> The Jefferson National Expansion Memorial was completed in 1965 to commemorate the westward expansion of hardy travelers and entrepreneurs. Known as the "Gateway to the West," the stainless steel arch cost $15 million to build and stands 630 feet tall. For a nominal fee, you can ride a small elevator to the top for a breathtaking view of St. Louis.

SIESTA MOTEL
CLOSE COVER BEFORE STRIKING

makers learned to love the highway. The endless horizon of telephone poles vanishing in the sun-swept distance provides a perfect backdrop for the grand vistas found on the widescreen canvas. To experience this widescreen fantasy in the early- to mid-century, many folks parked their cars in front of flickering outdoor screens to hear tinny speakers, crunch heart-clogging buttered popcorn, and maybe smooch a little. While the classic drive-in theater is being replaced by domed multiplexes with curved screens, stadium seating, and multiple shows per hour, you can still find sturdy reminders of simpler times along the highway, typically on land not yet fashionable to sell for redevelopment. One of the classic drive-ins, the 66 Drive-In Theatre in Carthage, was carefully renovated for a

1998 grand re-opening that was marked by a "film cutting" (as opposed to the more traditional "ribbon cutting"). Don't forget to cram into your car by nightfall, grab a soda and hot dog, and catch the flicks on 66.

While some travelers seek out the classic moviegoing experience, others flock with nearly cultish devotion to Carthage's major tourist draw, the Precious Moments Chapel. The Chapel celebrates those sweet doe-eyed figurines with a water-and-lights show, wedding facilities, and lots of gift shops. Touring the chapel is free, and worth a visit to view the lovely paintings and stained-glass windows, all featuring scenes from the Bible starring the Precious Moments characters.

MOONLIGHT MOTEL

West of Junction 71 By-Pass & 24 Highway
INDEPENDENCE, MO.

With its gurgling streams, distant peaks, and clouds like smoke from refineries churning toward the horizon, **Montana** stretches out in all directions. There was a time when the speed limits through the Treasure State were as fast "as prudence allows." But the folks in Big Sky Country decided that the sky is not the limit for racing and started enforcing the seventy-five miles per hour rule. A shame, perhaps, but now visitors are more likely to slow down when passing through Clinton, where the annual Testicle Festival revs up in September. Proving the adage, "Waste Not Want Not," the festival gathers a rowdy crowd of bikers, exhibitionists, road-trippers, and mellow locals to sample "Rocky Mountain Oysters": deep fried, beer battered bull testicles. Just like mom used to make.

Heading east toward Bozeman and Billings, take a break in beautiful Butte. Once called the most "wide open" town in the West, Butte was a magnet for saloons and whorehouses in the nineteenth

Mile-Hi Motel — in city limits, Butte, Mont.
32 Rooms

century. In the middle of it all, the longest continually running bordello in the United States put a classy spin on the oldest profession, and in more ways than one. The Dumas Brothel organized itself by class: the underground "cribs" facilitated quick, anonymous trysts; the main floor featured larger rooms and parlors for visiting miners

who had more change in their pockets; the upper story offered ornate suites to well-heeled gents. In its early decades, the Dumas ran twenty-four hours a day, servicing miners who emerged from the earth with a hankering for adult entertainment. The price for pleasure was fifty cents when the doors opened in 1890, and twenty bucks by closing time in 1982. Today, the Dumas struggles to redefine itself for less randy visitors. As an historic landmark, Dumas continues to revel in its sordid past, but recently appealed for a buyer to maintain this classic Victorian, attempting to sell the bordello on eBay for $75,000.

To the southeast in Gardiner, stop by the nearly seventy-year-old Jim Bridger Motor

With dazzling views of mountains, valleys, and snowdrifts, Going-to-the-Sun Road has been called one of the most scenic drives in the world. The fifty-mile-long passage carves through Glacier National Park and climbs over the Continental Divide to reach an elevation of 6,680 feet. Obstructed by snow during the winter months, the famed drive is worth the wait for spring.

Court — a site celebrating the greatest scout of the Rocky Mountains, according to the "Ripley's Believe it or Not" clipping framed in every log cabin. As the story goes, Jim sold a yoke of oxen for twenty-five dollars. In return, he got a volume of Shakespeare's works. Being unable to read, Jim then hired a wagon boy for forty dollars a month to read it to him. Jim also is credited with "discovering" the Great Salt Lake in 1824. Hop back onto the interstate to go eastward in search of Bozeman and the American Computer Museum. You may not think of computers when you think of Big Sky Country, but the folks in

Bozeman want you to rethink your definition of hardware and software. Their museum touts prehistoric cave artists as the first authors of the information age. The museum has collections of pebbles and stones from the first calculators, a telegraph, a nineteenth century Internet! The Computer Museum also includes "modern" computers whose punch cards and data tapes seemed futuristic not long ago. The price is right, especially if the kids are bored.

Nebraska was once known as the Great American Desert. Birthplace of Arbor Day, the Reuben sandwich, the 911 emergency system, and Kool-Aid, the Cornhusker State also serves as the home of Boys Town (now called Girls and Boys Town). At the Girls and Boys Town Hall of History just west of Omaha, you'll learn about the beloved site where Father Flanagan cared

PARK MOTEL

West Entrance to City   Steam Heated   SCOTTSBLUFF, NEBRASKA
Follow Highway No. 26, Short Cut to Yellowstone, All Oiled — See America's "Valley of the Nile"

for disadvantaged children. Opening his home to a handful of boys in 1917, Flanagan launched a crusade based on the belief that there are no bad boys, just bad circumstances. Boys Town became internationally known after Spencer Tracy won an Oscar for his portrayal of Flanagan in the 1938 film depiction of Boys Town. Today, you can visit a community that has grown considerably since its original handful of residents. And you can see the Academy Award garnered by an actor who played a saint.

Departing Omaha on Interstate 80, you'll surely want to drop by Lincoln to tour the state capital, study the statues of famous Cornhuskers, or perhaps visit a proper historical museum. Or maybe you'd rather see how folks could build a National Museum of Roller Skating. The museum will take you back to a time when gliding in circles around a stuffy rink while listening to organ music or maybe tunes from the jukebox offered the best way to spend a Saturday. The museum celebrates those memories with an impressive collection of memorabilia including a set of skates from 1819, artifacts from the first "Transcontinental Roller Derby," and exhibits exploring the rise, fall, and rebirth of in-line skates.

Back on the road, head west toward Elk Creek. As you head for the horizon, consider how Nebraskans share a particular appreciation of the automobile. State workers rushed to complete the interstate highway that weaves its lower third, completing their state allotment of the system before any other. Of course, Cornhusker

Omaha's Lied Jungle (pronounced "leed") contains the largest indoor tropical rainforest in the world. Re-creating climates from Asia, Africa, and South America, the 1.5 acre site allows visitors to glimpse waterfalls and exotic plant life. Visitors may also walk along an elevated pathway for a breathtaking treetop view of leopards, monkeys, and birds.

auto-appreciation pays special attention to a particular model. Nebraska celebrates the classic Chevy with a museum dedicated to the vehicle that provided millions of 1950s teenagers a chance to enjoy more than the cheesy movies showing at the drive-in. Located in Elm Creek on I-80, Chevyland, U.S.A., features over 110 restored and original Chevys built between 1914 and 1975. However, the most unique commemoration of the car may be found in northwest Nebraska near the town of Alliance. The best way to imagine this pavement pilgrimage site is to imagine how it came to be. Imagine that you're having a

family reunion, commemorating the passing of your father; you're struggling to find the appropriate monument to celebrate a life well lived. Naturally, you decide to build a Stonehenge out of cars. Well, that's what Jim Reinders and his family did. Their Carhenge monument stands near Alliance as a testimony to a peculiar vision of family, memory, and cars. As usual, locals hated the monument at first. Classify it as a junkyard, they said. But the tourists came by the tens of thousands, bringing their cameras and wallets, and now Alliance proudly proclaims itself the home of Carhenge.

Nevada was born silver and continues to mint gold. Once wealth was dug out of the ground, but today cash is removed from the wallets of visitors who ought to know better. Las Vegas lies in the heart of the empire. When the Pair-O-Dice Club opened on Highway 91, the Las Vegas Strip was born. Gangsters, molls, and desperados cheered the prospect of a "wide open" town in the middle of the desert. Of course, Las Vegas has long abandoned its wise-guy roots, crafting faux-visions of Paris, New York, and Renaissance Italy. But Las Vegas never forgets its roots, draw-

ing visitors who have cashed in their chips for the last time, too numbed by the clanking bells and flashing lights to care. After all, where else can you imagine a museum dedicated to Liberace? Featuring more candelabras than you can shake a candlestick at, the museum showcases dozens of rare pianos, glittering costumes, and outrageous automobiles such as the red, white, and blue Rolls-Royce convertible that showed Liberace's patriotic side.

Reno followed suit, but manages to stick closer to its hardwood, spit-stained, frontier past. Even the glossy hotel casinos that line the strip offer more functional facades than their cousins 450 miles away. There are lots of flashing lights and glaring colors, but there are no pyramids. As it happens, Reno and nearby Sparks still have their charms. For every tacky motel forced to deface itself for municipal uniformity in places like Anaheim, California, and Times Square, at least two neon throwbacks endure in Reno. Indeed, these folks know how to celebrate the starburst icon and sputnik light! Those quirky icons of the 1950s and 1960s, now stripped of their Cold War connotations, remain as prevalent as ever in this so-called "biggest little city in the world." Roll down Fourth (the Interstate 80 business loop) from the west side of town toward Sparks and get your camera ready: the Rancho Sierra and Farris

themselves after losing at cards. Others recall tales of local miners who'd struck it rich thanks to the Comstock Lode and then went so wild that the saloon-keeper cleaned up "buckets of blood" the next morning.

Motel (to the east of town) await. Along the way, check out the references to Highway 40. Before the age of interstates, the Victory Highway cut through Reno, not too far from the railroad. Stop by the Sparks Historical Society Museum to learn more; the folks there are plenty friendly. In Reno, you can stuff yourself at a buffet that resembles a Caribbean rainforest, but the $1.99 steak you may remember is history. As Nevada hotspots become more corporate, the penny pinchers save the great deals for those with deep pockets. If you're staying the night, the Sandman on Fourth is your best bet. You'll find rabbit ears on your TV, furniture out of a 1940's issue of *Better Homes and Gardens,* and no phones – but you'll also get a clean room in close proximity to the strip.

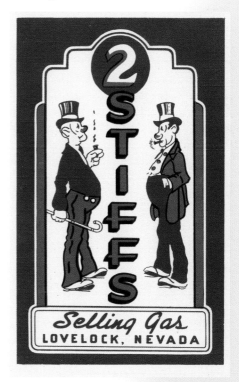

Nearby Virginia City once featured the Julia Bulette Red Light Museum, filled with nineteenth century sex tools, but now the site has been transformed into a lounge. Head down the street in search of the Bucket of Blood Saloon, where locals tell macabre stories of folks who killed

Every year folks visit **New Hampshire** in search of the fabled riot of orange and yellow to be found when the leaves turn in for the winter. During September and October, as the weather gets feisty, local townsfolk look forward to an influx of visitors who are delighted to purchase pricey trinkets and sleep in cozy bed-and-breakfasts. Once the last leaf has fallen, those same townsfolk are equally glad to enjoy some peace and quiet. Don't make the mistake of thinking that the Granite State has

only falling leaves to attract you, though. Where else can you experience "America's Stonehenge?" Plenty of places, actually. But this one was built over four thousand years ago, and, like its archeological cousin in England, can serve as an accurate calendar to forecast the cosmic dance of sun and moon.

Driving into Hillsboro, the birthplace of Franklin Pierce, you find none of the usual signs that celebrate a local hero. The quiet New Hampshire town, in fact, waited

about five decades to memorialize the fourteenth president at all. Such is fitting to a presidency marred by sadness and failure. Except for the Gadsden Purchase that led to statehood for Arizona and New Mexico, the Pierce Administration was simply dismal. Though blessed with charm, looks, and reasonable intelligence, Pierce ignored the imminent collapse of the Union by reportedly drinking his days away. At the end of his term, his own party abandoned him, and the nation careened toward civil war. The small Pierce Birthplace Museum balances this tragic history with more upbeat mementos, including a handwritten family tree that demonstrates the distant lineage between Franklin Pierce and the Barbara Pierce who eventually married our forty-second president, George Bush. You can also flip through a copy of Nathaniel Hawthorne's campaign biography featuring a foreword written by local students, who, in the municipal pride of an eighth grade class, explain that Pierce's reputation as one of the nation's worst presidents is most undeserved.

North a bit near the Daniel Webster Highway, you'll find Clark's Trading Post, an essential New England roadside attraction since its opening in 1928. The "trading post" name is a little misleading—Clark's has focused on animal attractions since its earliest days. Evolving from a

Tiny Town!

Further north, you'll find Bethlehem and the Crossroads of America. Visitors to this small community may not give Crossroads of America more than a passing glance, but slow down a bit. The nice folks inside would like to meet you, particularly if you love trains. Claiming to have the world's largest 3/16 scale model railroad, Crossroads presents a miniature world of mountains, tracks, yards, and highballin' locomotives that barely avoid the frightened robot cow that dares cross the track. Open since 1981, Crossroads of America delights visitors with about 300 feet of track in a three-story showcase for a single collector's boyhood dream.

trained-dog show, the post is now known mostly for its bear shows. However, you can purchase the assortment of trinkets and doodads you'd expect to find at a roadside stop. The North Woodstock site has also gathered bits and pieces from a defunct amusement park called Freedomland, so now it offers a train and ersatz main street.

Lined by 127 miles of beaches, boardwalks, and oceanfront towns, **New Jersey** has invited motorists since the beginning of the age of highways. The Garden State is best known to tourists as the home of Atlantic City, the fabled resort town of penny postcards and cotton candy where life is "peaches and cream." Of course, the reality of the city is dimmer than the bright hopes of that cheery song. For many

folks, the image of Atlantic City comes from the Burt Lancaster film of the same name. They envision decrepit tenements and glitzy casinos separated by overgrown blocks. Others might recall a Bruce Springsteen tune in which a desperate couple gambles for one last chance to head west where hope lies over the horizon. The truth lies somewhere in the middle of those extremes. At the Atlantic City

Historical Museum, there are all sorts of memorabilia related to the Miss America contest held off and on since 1921. The museum also includes a giant Mr. Peanut statue, a miniature boardwalk, and images from days when the town's million-dollar piers thronged with wax-mustachioed men and corseted women.

Heading south toward the kitschy, cool heart of New Jersey, you'll soon spot a towering pachyderm that has served as a Jersey landmark for more than a hundred years. Lucy the Elephant has bemused visitors to Margate since 1881 when she drew potential investors into New Jersey real estate. Potential catches would climb up to the howdah, a covered veranda of sorts, gaze out upon the thronging crowds, and imagine striking it rich in the Victorian housing boom. Since then, Lucy has served as a private residence, hotel, and a bar, among other things. Falling into disrepair in the 1960s, this landmark has since been rediscovered by local "Save Lucy" organizations and now invites motorists to dip their feet into the Atlantic next to the only pachyderm you can pass through alive.

Make your way south, through Ventnor and Ocean City. There, you'll find the kind of boardwalks worth driving to. There are helium balloons, kites, hot dog stands, and plenty of saltwater taffy. But it is the town

Did you know. . .

of Wildwood that offers a haven for lovers of neon and space-age "googie" architecture. If you're curious, googie is best described as a style in which the Flintstones meet the Jetsons. Some folks call it "populuxe" or even "doo wop," but googie best captures the coffee-shop ambience of gravity defying architecture, plastic palm trees, plate glass, atomic imagery, and 1950s fantasy come to life. The surf pounds the shore just a couple of blocks away from the strip which features roadside charmers such as the Pink Champagne

Motel with its marvelous neon sign, one of the original motor courts built before the crush of development in the 1960s. Nearby, the MarLane Motel invites visitors with its plastic globe lights that cast this site in a murky orange color. The pool glows like lime green Jello. You'll never forget your first drive down the Jersey Coast.

ELEPHANT HOTEL, MARGATE CITY
AN OLD LANDMARK, ATLANTIC CITY, N. J. — 7
THE ONLY ELEPHANT IN THE WORLD
YOU CAN GO THROUGH AND COME OUT ALIVE

New Mexico invites you to visit the "Green Chile Capital of the World," sample the world's largest enchilada, and tour the site of the first atomic bomb detonation. In other words, New Mexico is hot. Hot, dry, and absolutely charming. The state has long earned the respect of motorists for its indomitable roads and vast stretches of mesas and ghost towns. The "Land of Enchantment" also offers some of the nicest and best-maintained tourist courts in the country, particularly if you plan on sleeping in the fabled "land of 2000 rooms" — Tucumcari.

Tucumcari is one of those rare towns where the motel lights make you want to get out of the car and walk a while. The strip through town that used to be marked

Route 66 is a delight of blinking and glowing color. For many motorists, the heart of Tucumcari may be found in the Blue Swallow Motel. Until her death, Lillian Redman operated the Blue Swallow as an extension of her personal philosophy that all folks, even strangers, should try to help each other when they can. Mrs. Redman arrived in New Mexico by way of covered wagon in 1916, worked as a Fred Harvey Girl in her youth, and received the Blue Swallow as an engagement present in 1958. Even into her nineties, she offered a clean room, hardwood floor, and black and white television to road-weary travelers for eleven bucks and change. Her postcard offered an ancient prayer for travelers: "From 'birth 'til death' we travel between eternities. May these days be pleasant for you, profitable for society, helpful to those you meet, and a joy to those who know and love you best." With Redman's passing, the Blue Swallow fell under new ownership, but the old spirit remains.

Get a good night's sleep and get back on Route 66. But slow down and savor the moment when you reach Albuquerque, a cityscape of colorful murals where even the garbage bins are painted with angular coyotes and Zuni symbols. In the fall, you might spot hot air balloons painting a swath of colors across the sky. Cruise down Central Avenue to see about eighteen miles

You can actually drive on Route 666, if you don't fear its connotations as the "Devil's Highway."
Heading north from Gallup, the road was briefly featured in Oliver Stone's Natural Born Killers and consistently earns
rebuke from well-intended folks who demonize the highway supposedly numbered by the "mark of the beast."
As it turns out, the actual story of the devilish designation comes from highway planners who numbered the
road as the sixth branch from Route 66. Thus, Highway 666.

Heading south, you might want to tune your scanners for extraterrestrial signals if you plan to drive the alien highway toward Roswell. Since the 1947 crash of a purported UFO, Roswell has found itself in the crosshairs of various conspiracy stories. Supposedly the remains of alien visitors are located nearby. For a while, one imagines that local townsfolk tolerated outsiders but wished they could return to some peace and quiet. However, the town has lately decided to cash in. Since 1997, Roswell has hosted a UFO Festival during the Independence Day weekend that includes noted "ufologists,"an Electric Light UFO Parade, and costume contests. If aliens do show up, it's probably not wise to let them sample the green chiles.

of classic Route 66 businesses and some of the best neon in the southwest. Naturally, you'll want to stop at the 66 Diner for tasty shakes and gut-busting burgers. Be sure to say hello to folks who run decades-old courts such as El Vado Motel, Tewa Lodge, and Aztec Motel.

TEWA LODGE — ALBUQUERQUE, N. MEX.

New York City and its surrounding boroughs may justifiably be termed the capital of the world. Commerce, fashion, entertainment, and policy mix in marvelous and dazzling ways in the City that Never Sleeps. Of course, that mixture was never more potent than during the World's Fairs held in New York. World's Fairs represent hiccups in history when idealistic folks spin yarns of global unity — and entrepreneurial folks sell T-shirts and postcards. The bright beautiful tomorrow promised by the great fairs — a world of cheap energy, instant communication, and world peace — often becomes crystallized in theme buildings. Some of these structures, like the Eiffel Tower from the 1889 Paris Exposition, join the ranks of meaningful monuments. Others, like the 1982 Knoxville Sunsphere, are fortunate to show up in a *Simpsons* episode. The 1964-65 New York World's Fair Unisphere, located in Flushing Meadows-Corona Park, lies somewhere in between these extremes. The 140-foot tall steel Unisphere supposedly once represented the promise of international cooperation in the fields of space travel and telecommunication. More recently, the Unisphere has appeared in countless advertisements and was even blown up by a flying saucer in the 1997 film *Men in Black*.

WHEN IN NEW YORK BE SURE TO VISIT THE SHIP THAT NEVER GOES TO SEA

MIKE'S SHIP-A-HOY YACHT BAR "WHERE COLUMBUS MEETS BROADWAY AT 66th STREET, N. Y. C.

If you're going to drive a tollway, you might as well drive the longest, just to say you did. The 641-mile Governor Thomas E. Dewey Thruway is the longest toll superhighway in the United States, connecting New York City to Buffalo. The use of tolls was designed to ensure that the project could finance itself, with little tax burden on New Yorkers.

Tiny Town!

Located on the fairgrounds, the Queens Museum of Art offers a panorama of New York City, an overhead view of the metropolis in miniature. Composed of 275 four-by-ten-foot panels, the panorama includes 800,000 buildings and an airplane that departs regularly from LaGuardia airport, but no hint of traffic even in Times Square. Envisioned as a tool to aid city planners, the exhibit reminds its viewers of the breadth and vibrancy of America's First City. Walking around the panorama, don't be surprised when darkness falls and thousands of individually painted ultraviolet and phosphorescent paints, along with 2,500 lights, contribute to the illusion that night has overtaken the Big Apple. Today, you'll still find the Twin Towers as both a tribute to their eternal place in the New York skyline and as recognition of the reality that the panorama is updated very rarely. It serves as a snapshot of the five boroughs frozen in time. Glowing with an otherworldly beauty, the city is a child's toy of delights and an architectural celebration of the human spirit. Stick around and watch daylight return over Manhattan and the surrounding boroughs, and imagine the City that Never Sleeps facing a better day. Of course, there is more to see in the Empire State than the city which bears its name. For example, you may take the drive north to Troy and visit the actual gravesite

of Uncle Sam. You see, Uncle Sam was based on a Troy native who packed meat for soldiers during the War of 1812. Stamping the barrels with a "US," Sam earned the named Uncle Sam Wilson. Before long the white-haired character inspired by Wilson began to appear on postcards, cartoons, and other patriotic memorabilia signaling American resolve. If you prefer your heroes more lively than those found in graveyards, head north toward Lake Charles, where the world's tallest Uncle Sam is displayed.

Fast Food First!

North Carolina may be known for tar — in its nickname and in the tobacco products that help support the state's economy. But the state is also known for a much tastier treat. Krispy Kreme doughnuts were born in Winston-Salem in 1937 when Vernon Rudolph started selling the gluttomy-indacing confections through a cutout hole in his shop. Today, lines snake for blocks every time a new Krispy Kreme franchise opens its doors.

Of course, the Tar Heel State is known for all sorts of history. Its intimate relationship with the wind and water created a perfect combination for the world's first successful powered flight, now commemorated on the eternally evolving dunes. Nearby, like an artifact of an ancient society long lost to the sands of time, the miniature castle at Jockey's Ridge State Park provides an eerie reminder of the power of nature. Marking

the eighth hole of a miniature golf course now covered by the largest natural sand dune on the East Coast, the castle appears and vanishes depending on the wind. The dune itself moves like a living organism, covering about 400 acres by the beach. On gusty days, which are frequent, kite flyers and hang gliders ply the breezes in search

of the perfect combination of wind and fortune. Close by, you can walk on a path marked by stones where the Wright brothers took an even bigger chance with the fortunes of flight.

Heading inland past Greenville and Wilson, North Carolinians continue to seek the breezes for sport and pleasure. But few have turned the wind into an art form quite like Vollis Simpson. His home near Lucama displays a field of whirligigs — three-dimensional structures that spin and turn according to their balance and access to a good breeze. The best way to imagine a whirligig is to picture a huge mutated

White Lake, north of Elizabethtown, claims to be the "Nation's Safest Beach." Celebrated for its white sand, clear water, and utter lack of tides, the spring-fed attraction has attracted tourists since it was opened in 1901. Every May, locals hosts the White Lake Water Festival, complete with classic cars shows, tractor pulls, and live entertainment.

pinwheel sold at an extraterrestrial circus. While some whirligigs are tiny enough to fit in your hand, others tower over forty feet tall. Augmented with reflective parts, the whirligigs attract motorists day and night. Often prized as "folk art," Simpson's passion was featured at the 1996 Atlanta Olympics.

When driving the highways and byways toward the eastern half of North Carolina, you might pause to consider an important question: "Who is James Polk?" For many Americans, the question elicits an empty stare. But Pineville's James K. Polk Memorial wants to change all that. Within the compact presidential museum, you'll learn about Polk with the aid of displays, costumes, and political memorabilia. Older kids may enjoy the Nineteenth Century Notables interactive display, which challenges people to match the names of Polk's historical contemporaries with their pictures. Other displays convincingly demonstrate the impact of the "Spirited Age" on the United States, a nation transformed from the Jeffersonian cult of the rural farmer to the industrial age with its attending explosion in population and technological advances. When you're through, you'll have received a deeper appreciation for one of North Carolina's favorite sons.

White House Restaurant
U.S. Route 1 — Raleigh Road
HENDERSON, NORTH CAROLINA

North Dakota proudly launches U.S. 83-South, sometimes called "the Road to Nowhere." Plunging south through the plains toward Laredo, Texas, the highway dares you to pull off and head for a safer drive. Cruising past miles of empty expanse, you're left with little else but conversation to keep you company, even if it's with yourself. Perhaps in an effort to rid America of its limited perception of North Dakota as empty, frigid, and generally unappealing, state boosters have advocated

changing the name to simply "Dakota" for decades now. No one is quite sure how this new moniker would transform tourist perceptions of the Peace Garden State, so named for the botanical garden partly in North Dakota and partly in Manitoba beyond the Canadian border. But proponents of the new name are certain their efforts will eventually pay off. Until then, head north to the land of the Wild Prairie Rose anyway. There's plenty to see.

On the high plain as dusk begins to settle, the horizon seems to spill out in all directions. Half-glimpsed images, spectral phantoms of barely recalled pop culture icons, plant themselves in your subconscious. On the road to Regent, you're almost positive you spotted a five-story Teddy Roosevelt on horseback. Then you see a family of pheasants caught in three-dimensional metal splendor. Nearby, a similarly oversized giant grasshopper animates every

If you're the type of person who yearns to be in the center of it all, head for North Dakota. In the town of Rugby, you'll find the Geographical Center of North America marked by a stone "cairn." If you're not sure how to get there, look for the intersection of U.S. Highway 2 and North Dakota Highway 3, and you've hit the spot.

farmer's and B-movie fan's worst nightmare. Turns out, a local artist named Gary Greff envisioned an enchanted highway running about thirty miles between Gladstone and Regent, featuring one gargantuan structure after another, roughly every three miles. As you'd guess, the National Endowment for the Arts has gotten involved, offering Greff and his friends at North Dakota State University a grant to help build a "family metal park." Down the road, they imagine a golf course with metal trees and a youth ranch. Recently, Greff explained his new calling: "I have a vision. That vision is to make this why people say, 'I want to come to North Dakota.' "

Head a bit north to Dickinson to satisfy your kids' (or your own) passion for dinosaurs at the Dakota Dinosaur Museum. Just entering the site forces you past a ferocious looking Triceratops, which stands menacingly near the door. Inside, you'll find Velociraptor sculptures, a mural of a

Tyrannosaurus Rex, and an impressive collection of fossils. Like all great roadside attractions, this one began as a personal obsession. However, Larry and Alice League's private collection of dino-detritus outgrew its home and demanded more spacious digs.

Heading southeast toward the Coteaus and Prairies region, where glaciers once stood, stop by the Lawrence Welk Homestead in Strasburg, where the beloved bandleader was born in a sod house. The six-acre site contains original and period furnishings — and just maybe the echo of a million champagne bubbles ready to burst.

The eastern valley region offers a respite from driving in the form of Bonanzaville, USA, a twelve-acre museum complex of buildings that recreates life on the prairie. Documenting the intertwined lives of Native Americans and European-American settlers, Bonanzaville boasts over 400,000 historic artifacts.

A journey to the Buckeye State is a trip to the heart of America. Water sports, farmland, urban growth, suburban sprawl, country charm and big city culture all spread along gently undulating roads, rivers, hills, and plains. Roadside culture flourishes in **Ohio** in offbeat forms such as the Goodyear World of Rubber in Akron, the Airstream factory tour in Jackson Center, and the Kenneth Berger Hearing Aid Museum and Archives located at Kent State. You'll even discover the birthplace of a burger institution in the state's capital.

Fast Food First!

You see, try as he might, Dave Thomas just couldn't find a decent hamburger in Columbus, Ohio. So he looked back on the skills he learned while working at Kentucky Fried Chicken and decided to open a clean, reasonably priced hamburger joint in the middle of town. He named it after one of his daughters, Wendy. His grandmother taught him to never cut corners, so he kept his hamburgers square.

PARKWAY RESTAURANT — 18 PARK AVE. W., MANSFIELD, OHIO

Phone   **AMITY HOTEL COURTS**   7733
VALLEY 9536 ON U. S. HIGHWAYS 25 and 42 READING ROAD
FOR RESERVATIONS LOCATED AT NORTH CITY LIMITS CINCINNATI 37, OHIO

After Dave's death in 2002, America may have lost a homespun hero, but folks can still journey to the place where it all began. The museum filled with advertisements and other memorabilia is worth the drive. Sadly, Columbus has not shown reverence for all of its roadside attractions. Until its closing in 2000, the Kahiki Supper Club offered world-renowned Polynesian-style dining, pseudo-exotic ambiance, and dangerously fruity drinks. Entering through a pair of flaming Tiki gods, you'd find yourself in a darkly lit reproduction of a New Guinea men's meetinghouse filled with walls and quariums, artificial rainforests, and "mystery drinks" served by anonymous "island girls" whose presence would be announced by a loud gong. Given the ominous number of flaming icons, meals, and drinks, a writer for the Columbus Dispatch observed that "the Kahiki is one of the few restaurants in which the food can injure you." Today, lovers of the classic Kahiki bemoan its passing — demolished to make way for a drug store — but they wait for

The humble traffic light, the roadside sentry whose blinking eyes frustrate the speedy while ensuring the smooth flow of traffic, was born in London and raised in Detroit. But it took an African-American inventor named Garrett Morgan to liberate it from human hands. In 1923, he designed the first automatic traffic signal. Its first home was in Cleveland.

the gentle sway of ocean breezes to bring the Tiki spirit back to Columbus in the form of a new supper club to be built in the near future.

Head northwest to Toledo and stop by a classic café whose rumblings are not

Polynesian but Hungarian: Tony Packo's Cafe. For many folks, the first recollection of Tony Packo's Cafe comes from Corporal Klinger, the wacky company clerk in the long-running CBS hit *M*A*S*H*. In several episodes, Klinger celebrated the best (and technically, the first) Hungarian hotdog that ever graced a plate, available only in his hometown. Tony Packo's wasn't the stuff of television fiction, though; the Toledo eatery has served chili-cheese artery busters since the days of the Depression, when a factory worker decided to try his hand in the restaurant business. Now an essential Toledo stop, Tony Packo's celebrates its many celebrity diners with walls covered by over 1,000 hot dog buns signed by political figures, actors, and other notables. Stop by and try the "Chili Sunday": chili, sour cream, and cheese in a Sundae glass with warm chips on the side.

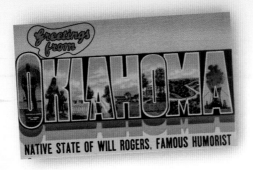

Greetings from OKLAHOMA

NATIVE STATE OF WILL ROGERS, FAMOUS HUMORIST

Oklahoma has been battered and bruised through the years, suffered booms and busts, but the Sooner State endures with a healthy mixture of humility, common sense, and gumption. For many folks, those qualities emerge most purely in the film *Grapes of Wrath* (1940), directed by John Ford. The movie provides a nearly perfect depiction of John Steinbeck's downtrodden Joad family's journey from Oklahoma dust bowl desolation to the fertile promise of redemption among the California orange groves. A battered truck, covered and filled with family and friends seeking a new life, illustrates the reality of countless people in the 1930s. Along the way, the Joads confront prejudice and fear among highway business owners and cops but also encounter big hearts and open arms from folks who recognize that the

STEAKS COOKED.... ....OVER CHARCOAL

Southwest's Most Unusual Steak House

Glen's HIK-RY INN

Charcoal Broiled STEAKS

2815 N.W. 10TH   WI. 3-4446 • OKLA. CITY, OKLA.

Close Cover Before Striking

word "Okie" is still shorthand for "American." The film's proto-socialist message may play a bit heavy-handedly to modern audiences, but its honest portrayal of hard-scrabble folks on Route 66, the Road of Flight, inspires tears, anger, and hope, all at the same time.

Along the remaining portions of Route 66 that pour across Oklahoma, local businesses strain to advertise some connection to the Mother Road, though their signs look brand new. If you're in the mood for something physical, you might pull off 66 for a bit and head east toward Stillwater. Advertising itself as the site where you can "feel the heat, smell the sweat and experience the excitement of ancient and modern wrestling," the Stillwater National Wrestling Hall of Fame struggles to remind

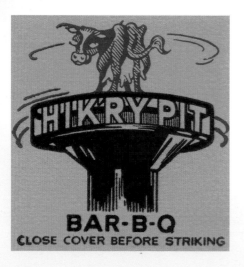

HIK'RY-PIT

BAR-B-Q

CLOSE COVER BEFORE STRIKING

its patrons about the difference between real wrestling and the silliness you'll find on television. Filled with memorabilia and dedicated to champions, coaches, and other folks who've helped maintain the dignity of mankind's oldest form of recreational combat, the hall of fame is worth the trip.

Back on the Will Rogers Highway, stop for a while in Oklahoma City and pay tribute to those who perished in the bombing of the Murrah Building. Head west out of town and the horizon opens up revealing an uncluttered sky, gleaming water towers, and marching telephone poles. In Yukon, the oft-photographed flourmill proudly advertises itself as the most modern in America. In El Reno, folks used to stop and scratch their heads. For a time, the Big 8 Motel advertised itself as "Amarillo's Finest." Had they gotten lost, or fallen asleep? No, the Big 8 was not located in Texas. However, when it was filmed as a backdrop for the 1988 film *Rain Man,* movie scouts thought this motel provided the perfect location, maps be damned. Now, the motel's name and sign have long changed, but the image persists in the flickering of movie memories.

Heading west, check out the Route 66 Museum in Clinton. Its audio tour (narrated by Michael Wallis, author of *Route 66: The Mother Road)* is augmented by musical selections from several decades of the Mother Road's existence and delightful exhibits of tourist courts, vacation spots, and diners. The folks in Elk City offer a respectable Mother Road Museum as well. Of course, regardless of which site you visit, you'll get a chance to chat with some of the finest people in the country.

Proclaiming itself the home of more ghost towns than any other state, **Oregon** draws visitors with its breathtaking coast and laid-back attitude. In The Beaver State, you can even sleep in a tree if you wish. On the southern border of Oregon, not too far from the Pacific Coast, Michael Garnier's Out 'n' About Treesort and Treehouse Institute offers a world famous bed and-breakfast located within the gently swaying branches of an oak grove in the Siskiyou Mountains. Of course, you'll have to do a bit of climbing to get into your room. Out 'n' About locates its facilities in more than a dozen tree houses with names like "Treezebo," "Serendipitree," and "Peacock Perch." For years, Garnier maintained his business out on a legal limb. County commissioners refused to grant a

permit for the facility out of concern for visitors' safety. Calling them "the tree stooges," Garnier responded by allowing guests to stay for free; they only had to purchase extravagantly priced T-shirts and promise to be good friends to the arbors. Today, Out 'n' About is legal and the guests keep coming in search of that perfect perch and unforgettable view.

Heading north past Pistol River along the Cape Sebastian State Scenic Corridor, you'll find some of the most awe-inspiring beaches in the world. Towering rock formations jut from waters that radiate azure, cyan, and turquoise as if all of Sedona, Arizona, had been flooded over a million years' time. Sea anemones are buffeted by the tides that strike the craggy coves while gulls glide and swoop on the air. Windsurfers and otters take to the waters while you skim the highway. In these parts, Highway 101 offers the usual assortment of inns, B&Bs, and seaside cottages, but few motels worth mentioning — with the exception of the Park Motel in Florence. This site, nestled among giant firs, is located near sand dunes and fresh water lakes. The coolest aspect of the Park, however, is the motel policy on dogs:

"Dogs are welcome in this motel. We never had a dog that smoked in bed and set fire to the blankets. We never had a dog who

stole our towels, played the TV too loud or had a noisy fight with his traveling companion. We never had a dog that got drunk and broke up the furniture. So, if your dog can vouch for you, you're welcome too."

Heading inland a bit, you might set your course for Gold Hill, but prepare to be perplexed. For some reason, the West Coast attracts more than its share of myste-rious alien visits and meteorite landings because of the proliferation of mystery spots, slanty shanties, and vortices. The curators of the Oregon Vortex near Gold Hill have maintained this tourist attraction and scientific oddity since 1904 but claim that Native Americans have long recounted narratives of freaky happenings. Visitors gasp when people and objects change height in relationship to the source of the mystery. Skeptics try to explain the phenomenon as a mere optical illusion, but their stories don't work at a campfire. By the way, don't call the Oregon Vortex a Mystery Spot (like the folks in California do). Curators explain that vortices, the underlying structure of the universe, are much cooler than spots.

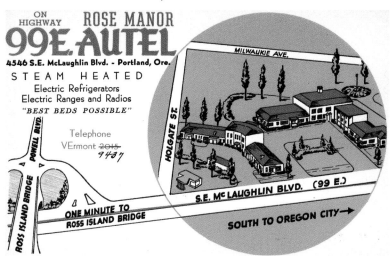

Pennsylvania is home to the first daily newspaper, the cheese steak sandwich, and is the chocolate capital of the world. The Keystone State is also the birthplace of a turnpike that popularized the notion of high-speed, all-weather highways whose limited grades and long straightaways helped inspire the postwar interstate highway system. But lovers of a certain windproof lighter will race north toward the New York border in search of the Zippo lighter museum. Since its founding in

Apple Valley VILLAGE SPECIALTY SHOPS

PANCAKE HOUSE

MILFORD, PIKE COUNTY · PENNSYLVANIA

1932, the company that manufactures Zippo lighters has crafted an American tradition of durability and collectibility. During World War II, journalist Ernie Pyle praised the lighter as an essential battlefield accessory, saying that it "is the most coveted thing in the Army." Today, you can visit the Bradford Pennsylvania Zippo Museum, visitor center, and repair site where they'll fix your Zippo for free. The 15,000-square-foot museum features a 7-by-11-foot American flag composed of red, white,

and blue Zippo lighters. If you're lucky, you'll also spot the Zippo car, a refurbished 1947 Chrysler Saratoga topped by two larger-than-life Zippo lighters spouting neon flames.

Tiny Town!

Since 1953, Shartlesville's Roadside America has attracted folks with an eye for tiny craftsmanship and big dreams. A series of villages representing America from coast to coast, Roadside America includes two centuries of history in the design styles of its miniature homes, businesses, and amusements. It was born when five-year-old Laurence Gieringer stared at a far-off hotel from his window, imagining it to be a tiny toy just out of reach. Setting out in search of the toy, little Laurence quickly became lost. A frantic night ended with searchers discovering the frightened boy, who promised he'd never run off like that again. But the dream of that little toy took hold, and Laurence soon started building his own tiny buildings: hotels, churches, farmhouses, eventually an entire village. Local attention inspired by a newspaper article spread across the state and eventually the country. Laurence realized his calling and created what stands today as an over-8000-square-foot fantasy world where the Statue of Liberty and the Sermon on the Mount compete for your attention with a

Pittsburgh claims bragging rights to the world's first drive-up automobile service station. Built in 1913 to resemble a pagoda, the Gulf Refining Company service station offered more than just gas; you could purchase oil and other lubricants, put air in your tires, and even use the employee restroom. Today the station exists only as a memory and a commemorative plaque.

MILFORD, PENNSYLVANIA
Established 1928

MILFORD *Diner*

GATEWAY TO PIKE COUNTY'S VACATIONLAND...

miniature movie theatre playing *Boys' Town.*

Next, visit the Eisenhower home, accessible from the sprawling Gettysburg tourist trap complex where mammoth tour buses pass by wax presidents, ghost sites, and even one of the few cycloramas remaining to project time on a curved painting. From the Gettysburg National Park Service Visitor's Center, you'll catch a bus that

drives about seven miles to the Eisenhower farm, where former president Dwight Eisenhower loved to show heads of state his prized collection of cattle. After the docent's overview, you're free to tour the house with a handout to summarize each room. The farm was the only home ever purchased by Dwight and Mamie Eisenhower and served as their retirement home. After Dwight's death in 1969, Mamie lived on the farm for another ten years, greeting visitors and conducting correspondence from her bed until noon — for she believed that a woman of a certain age earned that privilege. In the afternoon, she enjoyed watching soap operas in the sunroom, unless she was hosting a bridge game or gathering of one of her clubs. Then, a Secret Service agent would watch the show, taking copious notes to be sure the former first lady would not miss any details from her favorite shows. Walking through a hallway, you can even pick up one of the presidential phones — a friend might have called Ike at Edgewood 4-4454.

Rhode Island, home for over a million folks along the Atlantic Coast, has struggled with its tourist image. In 2000, state officials placed forty-seven six-foot-tall Mr. Potato Head statues around the Ocean State to celebrate Rhode Island's status as home to the company that manufactures the beloved spud. With a crop of potato statues, each designed to represent the whimsical vision of local artists, out-of-towners surely would visit the "Birthplace of Fun!" Unfortunately, the "Tourist Tater" drew the wrath of a small number of folks

The stainless steel diner is a gleaming, streamlined refuge from the working day. Wiping away the sweat and grime of factory life, a diner patron could order a greasy burger and a chilled soft drink. After a late shift, a working person could straddle a rotating stool and nurse a cup of joe. The server might have been on her feet for twelve hours collecting nickels and dimes, but she'd be glad to hear your story for a moment and maybe bring you a plate of pie with a dollop of ice cream. The classic American diner, celebrated in film and tel-

GREETINGS FROM
PAWTUCKET
RHODE ISLAND

who thought the dark-skinned, Hawaiian shirt-wearing mascot appeared to mimic racist stereotypes. Even so, you can tour Rhode Island in search of those statues not yet sold for charitable purposes and try to remember that the state may be small, but the fun is big-time. Along the way, you'll discover a diner museum in the making and a classic store that endures.

evision, emerged in Providence when Walter Scott converted a horse-drawn wagon to a rolling chow hall in 1872. More than a century later, the American Diner Museum has nearly completed construction of a tourist attraction celebrating this cultural landmark. When it opens, the museum will showcase advertisements, matchbooks, photographs, and other diner artifacts. It will also have a working

Depression-era diner, built by the Worcester Lunch Car Company, that visitors can tour.

Turning northwest toward the Connecticut border, plan to visit an essential New England stop: an honest-to-goodness general store. In a growing country, when distances were truly vast, the small shop had to offer a little bit of everything — including conversation and a chance to catch up with the news of the day. When's the right time for planting? What's the chance of bad weather coming through? Where's a decent place to catch a fish dinner? The general store offered locals and travelers alike a chance to sit down and rest a spell. If you're going to visit one, it might as well be the oldest. Set in the heart of Rhode Island's Blackstone Valley, "birthplace of American industry," the Brown and Hopkins Country Store in Chepachet has operated continually since 1809. Even today, you can grab a cup of coffee and warm up next to a pot-bellied stove. Of course, you'll quickly notice the boutique-y vibe as recent owners have sought to attract the weekend shopping crowd from the surrounding outlet malls. But for simple down-home history, the Hopkins Country Store maintains a tenuous hold on a rapidly receding past.

MONKEY ISLAND, ROGER WILLIAMS PARK, PROVIDENCE, R. I.

South Carolina may be known as the starting point of the "War Between the States," and it can surely take pride in a tourist destination like Myrtle Beach that claims to be the miniature golf capital of the world, but the Palmetto State also advertises itself as the peach capital of the world. Here, trouble brews. Folks to the south in Georgia and Alabama may disagree, but South Carolinaians boast the "peachoid" to prove their case. Sure, you may find other peach-shaped water towers — Alabama sports one that's pretty big — but the Gaffney peachoid stands tallest, holding one million gallons of water. The key is to ignore the nagging sensation that the peachoid is really a giant rear-end mounted near Interstate 85. Once you get that mental image out of your brain, the peachoid is worth the drive.

Head southeast for Charleston, a community of quaint shops, bountiful antique stores, and tangible history. Also, you'll find a museum to set your teeth on edge. The Macaulay Museum of Dental History provides a tribute to teeth cleanings, root canals, and all of the other delightful experiences associated with oral hygiene. Like most museums of this sort, this one grew from the personal obsession of a Palmetto State dentist who gathered his collection of

Pocalla Springs Tourist Court and Swimming Pool, 3 Miles South of Sumter, S. C.,   U. S. Hy. 15A

New Community Building, Laundry, Showers, Shuffleboard and horseshoe courts for Trailer Guests. All Guests have free access to swimming pool and good fishing.

M. H. Beck, O. M. Hill, Managers and Owners, Telephone 3602

65166

instruments over several decades. The museum has all the makings of a nine-teenth-century dental office, proving vividly how far the art and science of dentistry has come. You'll find yourself oddly in-trigued by early x-ray units, teeth molds, and even a bill for services rendered.

Cruising toward the northern edge of South Carolina, South of the Border is impossible to miss as "Frito Bandito" cari-catures entice motorists with catch phrases like "You never sausage a place!" and "Chili Today - Hot Tamale!" In an age of political correctness, South of the Border is unapologetic. The motel's mascot, Pedro, leers into the face of polite society — dar-ing you to get offended. No doubt, many

do. Right after you pass the billboard that instructs, "Keep yelling at kids! They'll stop," Pedro appears, hoisting a giant sign and standing ten stories tall. Turning onto U.S. 301, you enter a neon nether world of shops, restaurants, amusements, and — oh yes — 300 motel rooms. After getting your room key, a teenager guides you with his bicycle through the maze of streets to your door. Just follow "Pedro," the clerk says. Supposedly all the employees of this complex are called Pedro. Nearby, other-worldly electric cacti glow and hum. Pedro salt and pepper shakers are on sale. Want some fireworks, T-shirts, sex toys, or maybe a round of indoor golf? You'll find these wonders at South of the Border, under a 200-foot sombrero tower. There are even twenty so-called heir-conditioned honeymoon suites: "When Nothing but the Very Best Will Do for the Bride!" Wandering the many stores found in the complex, you'll find souvenir spoons, cups, pennants, back-scratchers — just about any cheap and tacky way to remember your stay.

South Dakota must respect Idaho's position as America's potato king, but do those spud-suckers to the west wrestle in the stuff? Every year, the valiant folk of Clark, celebrate Potato Day by filling wading pools with mashed potatoes and practicing their best Greco-Roman moves. The tradition simply proves that life in South Dakota isn't all flat and dry. Sometimes it's lumpy and wet. Even so, they don't call it the Mount Rushmore State for nothing.

At one point in your life, you simply must head out toward the Black Hills National Forest to see the monument to Presidents Washington, Jefferson, Lincoln, and Theodore Roosevelt. It's hard to tell whether this tourist attraction is a monument to presidential kitsch or is "the formal rendering of the philosophy of our government," as envisioned by builder Gutzon Borglum. Twenty-five miles south of Rapid City, Mount Rushmore is certainly worth the drive. For nineteen bucks a carload, you can also visit the Crazy Horse Memorial. Its unofficial slogan is "you can-

not experience the Crazy Horse Memorial by driving past on the highway." The towering statue of the Native American hero has been under construction since 1948 and promises to be the site of a university, medical school, and airport. Because the monument is built with the aid of private donations — with no state or federal assistance — there is no assurance that Crazy Horse will fully emerge in our lifetimes.

Heading east along Interstate 90, you're about to visit one of the great roadside attractions of the Midwest. Wall Drug is the sprawling gem of the Badlands that reminds the roadside tourist of South of the Border in South Carolina. Within its several blocks of storefront, you can see a mechanical T-Rex, impress your significant other at the shooting gallery, ride the giant jackalope, and pose next to a faux Mount Rushmore. Selecting from the hundreds of postcards and literally thousands of knick-nacks, it's hard to believe that this was once a tiny drugstore in a prairie town of 326 people. In a pamphlet that tells the history of this incredible place, Ted Hustead (recently deceased) recalls that an offer of

Rated No. 3 Among U. S. Caves
The Old Original, World's Greatest

CRYSTAL CAVE "IN THE BLACK HILLS" SOUTH DAKOTA

Be Sure About the Location
On 14 and 79, Halfway Between Piedmont and Tilford

free ice water was the difference between survival and defeat for the struggling store: "It brought us Husteads a long way and it taught me my greatest lesson, and that's that there's absolutely no place on God's earth that's Godforsaken. No matter where you live, you can succeed, because wherever you are, you can reach out to other people with something that they need!"

Before completing your journey, probably in Sioux Falls, take a break in Mitchell, where there's a world doll museum, a prehistoric Indian village, and a museum dedicated to the creation of the border between the Dakotas. But you know why you've come. You're here to see the Corn Palace, all five stories of it. Built originally in 1892 and rebuilt a couple of times since then, the Corn Palace features a façade completely covered by corn and its allies: grain, oats, rye, straw, wheat, and other symbols of South Dakota's agricultural roots. Every year, local artists engage in an eternal struggle against persistent blackbirds, covering the palace with images depicting the role of agriculture in South Dakotan life and addressing other unique themes. Recently, the palace displayed famous images of American history over a faux website: www.millennium.corn.

THE WORLD'S ONLY CORN PALACE, MITCHELL, S. D.
Original cost $275,000.00. Redecorated annually at a cost of $10,000.00 in corn, grains and grasses. The most marvelous exhibit of nature's wonderful colors blended into works of classic art by skilled decorators.

Tennessee may be home to Davy Crockett, Casey Jones, and Minnie Pearl, but the Volunteer State's most significant pop culture resident was a shy man from Mississippi named Elvis Presley. It's difficult to explain the impact Elvis Presley had on American popular culture, though countless books and articles have tried. In 1968, one observer wrote that if any music could bleed, this was it. Pulling together a tapestry of lyrical and rhythmic threads from the deep South, Elvis was more than a rock star; he embodied the overlapping innocence and sin of the postwar United States. A few years back, Paul Simon captured the feeling of that divide and the distant dream by singing, "Maybe I have reason to believe we all will be received in Graceland." Going to Graceland is part guilty pleasure and part civic duty. We are drawn through its wrought-iron music-note gates even when the thrill of hearing the King blare through the radio has long subsided. For the visiting faithful, Graceland provides the chance to visit the Jungle Room, gaze upward in a cathedral

of accolades, and unravel the mysteries of Elvis' obsession with peanut butter and banana sandwiches.

Another Tennessee export changed the world in a far different way. Launched in Memphis, Holiday Inn promised low prices, consistent quality, and convenient locations to a generation of Americans heading out for the highway. Holiday Inn began as the vision of Kemmons Wilson in 1952 after a road trip gone bad. Driving to Washington, D.C., on a family vacation, Wilson grew frustrated at the lack of quality he found in roadside motels. Dingy courts and dusty motor hotels may have been satisfactory when Americans first set out on the road, but Wilson was sure the interstate age would call for new kinds of amenities: air conditioning, restaurants, in-room telephones, and — most of all — standardization.

His first Holiday Inn, built on Summer Avenue in Memphis, was so successful that Wilson followed up with identical ones on three other roads leading into Memphis. By 1972, his company franchised 1,405 inns in the United States and around the world, and Wilson was featured on the cover of *Time* magazine. Before long, however, a corporate mentality shifted Holiday Inn's attention away from family motorists and toward well-heeled business-class

ALHAMBRA COURTS
WEST OF KNOXVILLE, TENN. RECOMMENDED BY DUNCAN HINES (AAA)
ON 11 AND 70

travelers. They even abandoned the forty-three-foot "great sign" for a less boisterous backlit model. Today, Kemmons Wilson's vision is best found on dusty postcards.

Before you hit the highway to leave the Volunteer State, stop and pay your respects at the Buford Pusser Home and Museum, located in Adamsville. Part-time professional wrestler, one-time bear wrestler, Buford is known to most folks through the *Walking Tall* film series which depicted the McNairy County sheriff who endured shootings, stabbings, and even the killing of his wife while he did his duty busting

up moonshiners and other hoods. Pusser himself died under mysterious circumstances. The Pusser home features the furniture and other memorabilia of the Tennessee peace officer whose beat got plenty violent.

Greetings from
TEXAS
THE LONE STAR STATE

Texas demands respect. Occupying the largest area in the southern forty-eight states and boasting an historical state marker seemingly every five feet, Texas shows no lack of self-confidence. For many folks, the richest memories of Texas come from the writings of Larry McMurtry. For others, the television show *Dallas* pretty much sums it up. When you arrive, plan to stay a while — the Lone Star State really is "like a whole other country."

The Mother Road traverses about 175 miles of Texas Panhandle and, as Bobby Troup wrote, "you'll see-ee-ee Amarillo." But you'll dream of seventy-two ounces of steak: a solid two inches of sirloin heart attack flanked by a baked potato, salad,

shrimp cocktail, and roll. Oh, and it's free if you can consume the entire meal in one hour. Otherwise, you're out about fifty bucks — and no one will want to drive home with you.

Heading west, crane your neck to the left and you'll spot ten Cadillacs jutting out of the earth. You'll wonder why. Why did a group called Ant Farm purchase the cars ranging from a 1949 Club Coupe to a 1963 Sedan just to bury them in a wheat field? Why did members of Ant Farm respond to one of the Caddies' owner's exorbitant price of 700 bucks for the car by purchasing the car only to smash its front end with sledgehammers? Why did a helium-business millionaire named Stanley

CROCKETT COURT
Overlooking the Gulf of Mexico
4214 AVE. U - GALVESTON, TEXAS

Lone Star State trivia buffs often surprise their friends by announcing that Texas is the only state added to the union by treaty as an independent republic, and that the Texas state flag may fly at the same height as the United States flag. Both claims are incorrect. Hawaii, California, and Vermont were considered separate "nations" before admission. The Texas flag code also states clearly that the Texas flag must fly a respectful distance below the United States flag.

March 3 (definitely not "the third") sponsor the project? Wonder first, then wander there. Bring spray paint and paint your message. Ant Farm intended their Cadillac Ranch to provide a performance art piece for passing motorists, and a chance to reflect on some deeper meaning.

Cruise south into the heart of Texas and dream of the sweet and slightly kicky taste of Dr Pepper. Can one describe its particular variant of taste and attitude? For years, folks have tried to capture this sensation in a bottle, unleashing an Attack of the Pepper Clones. One webpage keeps track of Pepper-partners that include Dr. Becker, Dr. Buzz, Dr Skipper, and the creepy-sounding Dr. Smooth. But the real Dr Pepper was introduced to a global audience at the 1904 St. Louis World's Fair. For years, folks have turned to the good doctor in search of a non-cola caffeine high. Even so, the taste changed when corporate Pepper-suits decreed that the soft drink would be bottled with cheap corn sweetener. A Dublin, Texas, bottler, known locally as "Mr. Dr Pepper," stuck with Imperial Pure Cane Sugar. Today, thousands of folks a year journey from around the world to sample the tooth-eating ambrosia, confident of Dr Pepper's medicinal properties. The Dublin bottling plant offers tours (most Tuesdays are bottling days), maintains a swell collection of Pepper memorabilia, and even features an old-fashioned soda fountain.

Before leaving the Lone Star State, don't forget to stop in Dallas to remember the assassination of JFK. The Sixth Floor Museum at Dallas' Dealey Plaza succeeds in portraying the Kennedy administration's final days and its shaken aftermath with balance and tact. It addresses the potential of conspiracy in the shooting of the president admirably. A critical look at the Warren Commission report is balanced by an overview of various conspiracy theories that point the blame at the FBI, CIA, the mob, Cubans, Soviets, right-wingers, and several others.

In some early travel cards, you might spot a "See America First" billboard. The slogan refers to a western booster movement that blossomed throughout the first three decades of the twentieth century. Even Cole Porter tried to capitalize on the movement with his 1916 musical of the same name that featured a tune called "Will You Love Me When My Flivver is a Wreck?" As this tune reminds us, the realities of offering tourist destinations to the hardy traveler.

As it has since its settlement, Salt Lake City offers a comfortable respite for weary motorists, particularly those interested in the history of the Latter-day Saints. People cannot tour the Mormon Temple, unfortunately. You'll be told it's not secret but sacred. Yet you can get an earful of heaven-

HOME SWEET HOME WAS NEVER LIKE THIS

highway life — the unimproved two lane roads and the vast distances between mechanics — brought many auto-expeditions to a grinding halt. However, decades before, a vast stretch of struggle and hardship also brought a group of Mormon pioneers to the Great Basin where they built a temple, settled a territory, and embarked on the path toward statehood. **Utah** has changed much since those pioneer days, integrating its self-proclaimed peculiar people into the fabric of the nation, and ly music if the Mormon Tabernacle Choir is in town. Or you can tour Temple Square, where eager and earnest missionaries just love to chat with visitors. If religious pursuits don't interest you, there's always Salt Lake's "Gravity Hill," an optical illusion like any number of mystery spots and freaky vortices that appear to break the laws of physics. Naturally, this cosmic conundrum is located a few blocks from the state capital.

Visitors to Levan, Utah, confront yet another wacky story for the origin of the town's name. Historians point out that Levan (or "Le Van") refers to a rear rank of an army or a frontier settlement. Local folks out to tickle your funny bone tell another story. Levan got its name as a backward spelling of "Navel." Unbelievable? Look at the map; Levan does lie in the center of the state.

East of Salt Lake, near the Colorado border, you'll find one of the truly great signs ever to grace the roadside: the Dine-A-Ville that used to welcome visitors to Vernal with batting eye lashes and an imaginary roar. The friendly forty-foot tall dinosaur came close to extinction when her home motel was demolished, but townsfolk and other lovers of "Dinah" moved her across town where she stands tall.

There's no easy way from Vernal south to Moab, but getting there puts you on the set where Ridley Scott's *Thelma and Louise* (1991) met their tragic and controversial end. Part of the power of this film may be found in the cinematography, in which lonely mesas, snorting 18-wheelers, and miles of blacktop formed the backdrop for a drama in which a waitress and housewife hit the highways after killing a would-be rapist. Finding no hope on the road, Thelma and Louise turn to each other, even as they turn to crime. Terrifying and even comic moments of violence intersect long leisurely stretches of driving as the two desperados head west in a '66 Thunderbird.

Taking a more leisurely course, you'll end up in Four Corners, USA, where Utah, Colorado, New Mexico, and Arizona form the only point in which four states meet. You'll endure the heat and even some traffic, pay the small fee, take the picture in which you straddle the magical marker, and then get back on the road.

Vermonters don't care much for wasted speech. Consider the story of Calvin Coolidge, a man who best illustrates the Green Mountain State's attitude toward loquacious folks. While at a party, a socialite approached the fellow known as "Silent Cal" and said that she'd made a bet that she could convince the reticent speaker to utter more than three words. He replied, "You Lose."

To really understand his brand of humor, you must cruise through groves of hard pine to the hamlet of Plymouth Notch, **Vermont**. President Calvin Coolidge State Historic Site is one of the most satisfying stops you'll make because it so faithfully retains the small town feeling that shaped the character of the man who served as America's thirtieth president.

Adding perfectly to the quiet state's emphasis on somber meditation as an alternative to the manic activities practiced virtually everywhere else along the roadside, imagine just how relaxing the American Museum of Fly Fishing must be. Located in Manchester, the museum features artwork, literature, and a world-renowned collection of artifacts related to the mellow pursuit. The array includes hand-tied flies and other fishing equipment that belonged to folks like Babe Ruth, Daniel Webster, and Bing Crosby.

For a more light-hearted taste of Vermont, head north toward Waterbury and catch the Ben & Jerry's ice cream tour. You'll learn about the social activism that gets whipped into every scoop of Cherry Garcia, Chunky Monkey, and Phish Food ice cream. Free taste samples are the highlight of the factory tour, along with a brief film depicting the history of two childhood friends who renovated a gas station in 1978 to sell ice cream and advocate for social justice. Giving away over a million dollars a year, Ben & Jerry's supports causes that range from the creation of eviction-free zones to the protection of endangered wetlands. The tour is cheap and the ice cream is great.

Further northward toward the Canadian border, you might pass through Danville and feel an attraction for a small museum and headquarters of a group called the American Society of Dowsers. Trust that instinct and let supernatural forces guide the wheel as you discover the site. Dowsing, you may recall, involves the use of an instrument such as a forked stick to search for underground water. Of course, hard-core dowsers will quickly remind you of their ability to discover all sorts of bizarre phenomena including electromagnetic fields and minerals, along with "noxious rays and geopathic zones." The museum contains a tiny exhibit and shop where you can purchase your first L-rod, Y-rod, or auremeter.

Completing your Vermont tour, take the tiny roads west through the Green Mountains, home of Revolutionary fighters such as Ethan Allen who forced the surrender of British Fort Ticonderoga. Returning to the interstate, don't be surprised to find two thirteen-foot-tall whale tails sticking out of the ground near Randolph. The black granite sculpture, titled Reverence, has struggled for a permanent home since the developer who commissioned it abandoned the project years ago.

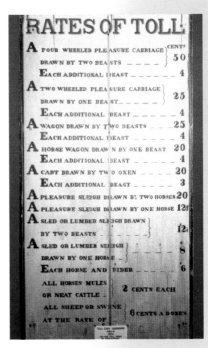

Virginia has been called the birthplace of presidents since eight men who occupied the nation's highest executive office were born amongst its green hills and verdant valleys. Within one extraordinary day, you could tour the narrow passageways and gorgeous views of George Washington's Mount Vernon, visit James Madison's Montpelier with its stunning panorama of the Blue Ridge Mountains, and see the stately home of William Henry Harrison. With a good map and a lead foot, you could even squeeze in quick visits to histor-

ical sites (or historical markers, at least) dedicated to James Monroe, Zachary Taylor, and Woodrow Wilson. Don't get too excited about the Taylor monument, though. It's just a sign along a state road. Two Virginia presidential sites are worth special attention: Thomas Jefferson's Monticello and John Tyler's Sherwood Forest.

Thomas Jefferson's Monticello offers a testament to the happy confluence of interests, hobbies, and passions that animated the red-haired Virginian. Touring the house allows you to gaze over a small portion of Jefferson's collection of paintings, scientific instruments, maps, and prehistoric bones. It seems that when Jefferson sent Lewis and Clark westward, he really wanted them to find mastodons. Your tour guide may cheerfully remind you that Jefferson was about 10,000 years too late. Stepping into Jefferson's more personal spaces, even his bedroom where he slept in an alcove, you can recollect how folks remembered their loved ones before the advent of photography. You will see dozens of silhouette images of Jefferson's friends and family members. Jefferson's eye for design includes a multitude of octagonal rooms built to reduce the accumulation of shadows. However, their design also ensures an occasional claustrophobic feeling as visitors bunch up in several bottlenecks. After the formal tour, walk through the gardens at a slower pace, savoring the pungent aroma of eggplant, green pepper, and lavender.

Southeast of Monticello, former president John Tyler built a home in Charles City. The manse was called Sherwood Forest after fellow Whig Henry Clay named Tyler an outlaw for defying his adopted party's nationalist agenda. However, Tyler was no

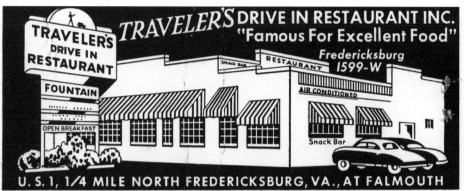

ruffian. His aristocratic lineage displays itself in his home, the largest frame house in the United States. The house occupies land the length of a football field. The half-hour tour includes fascinating background narrative by a well-rehearsed docent who points out intriguing details such as the spot where Union soldiers set fire to a hallway table, seeking to burn the mansion down after former president Tyler joined the Confederacy. Fortunately, the captain of a passing Union gunboat recalled Civil War promises to safeguard presidential homes, but not until after the place was looted and a looking glass was shattered to make soldiers' shaving mirrors. Stepping into the west "hyphen" of the building, you enter a long thin room where the Tyler family would host "blow outs" — all night parties that only ended when the last candle was extinguished. While he and his wife enjoyed the Virginia Reel, Tyler's daughter fancied the then-vulgar waltz. Leaving the grounds, visit a pet cemetery with stone statues of patriot dogs, cats, and a duck.

Washington State may be known for its apples, its empire of Starbucks coffee houses, and a software company that still does Windows, but roadside aficionados visit the Evergreen State in search of Zillah's Teapot Dome Service Station, considered by some historians to be the oldest continually running gas station in existence. Built in 1922 and located near Yakima, the station commemorates the infamous scandal of the same name through its construction as a huge teapot. Historians recall the Teapot Dome Scandal as a revelation of government corruption when public lands were used for private gain during the Harding administration. Thank goodness that never happens anymore! Get a tank of gas and you might drive further south toward Maryhill to find a memorial to America's World War I dead. It happens to be a replica of Stonehenge because its creator thought the original was a sacrificial site. Despite its mistaken inspiration, the Washington State Stonehenge is worth a visit.

Heading northward, one may shoot west toward Seattle or east in search of Spokane. Starting in Seattle, you can visit the location where the 1962 World's Fair introduced a 520-foot Space Needle to the world. The famed needle sells all sorts of trinkets and doodads in its windowed ring, providing gorgeous views of the thriving metropolis nearby and majestic Mount Rainier to the southeast. A portion of the monorail, that promised a fantasy world of fluid transportation, built by Disney, continues to trundle barely a mile from point to point. The city offers a handful of intriguing stops, including a telephone museum and a collection of petroliana.

But the road calls before long. Out on U.S. 2, cruise east toward Leavenworth, a Bavarian-themed city where every dwelling is a haus and every hill is alive with the sound of music. Naturally, you'll want to stop at the Alpen Inn Motel. But also visit the Timberline Motel with its stone cottages — each individually named for local trees like Juniper, Fir, and Cypress. Even

this far east of Seattle, Washington, reminds you of its identity as espresso capital of America with its many roadside coffee stands and "chalets." Further along, the Valley Cottage Motel rests near the cascading Wenatchee river and an apple orchard. Past Lincoln Rock State Park, Highway 2 empties out into a glimmering desert of scrub, heat mirages, and dust devils. Near Coulee City, you'll find the Ala Cozy Motel where the pool is advertised as "our only liquid asset." There are no evergreen trimmings or freshly painted shutters at this site. The Ala features a weather beaten mini-golf city with its own saloon, jail, and chapel.

Racing toward Spokane in summertime, the cool Pacific breezes recede pretty quickly. Rest awhile at Riverfront Park, site of the 1974 World Expo. It may be hard to remember, but a couple of generations ago, folks viewed World's Fairs and Expositions like the one held here as exemplars of civilization, the height of human ingenuity.

More than two decades after the expo closed in Spokane, you can still stroll under the wings of an artificial butterfly and peer up at the fair's clock tower. Nearby, climb an almost-two-story Radio Flyer sculpture commissioned by the town's Junior League. Visitors race up the steps and slide down the "handle." Locals offer knowing smiles as they walk past.

OUR WAY HOME
AFTER VISITING
THE SPACE NEEDLE

Covered with forests, flowing with white-water rafting, and glistening with ski slopes, **West Virginia** offers plenty to attract hardy travelers. The Eastern Panhandle reminds you of the Mountain State's role in colonial and Civil War history. There is even a town named after George Washington's brother, Charles. Within its valleys and mountain regions, West Virginia provides all the typical tourist attractions: glass blowing, bed-and-breakfasts, and antiquing opportunities that will strain any credit card. The

Mountain State also provides an attraction you won't find anywhere else: the 112,000-square-foot atomic bunker where the members of the Cold War-era United States government would relocate in case of nuclear attack. The site — located under the Greenbriar Hotel in White Sulphur Springs — was closed in the 1990s.

Oddly enough, many of the coolest roadside attractions may be found in the Northern Panhandle. Driving through West Liberty, you might notice a school bus with black and white photograph passengers that gaze out the windows. These folks are famous women who advocated reform, struggled for suffrage, and made a difference. The Women's History Museum is a unique educational experience because it can come to you. Robert and Jeanne Schramm, the team operating this rolling exhibit, love nothing so much as arriving at schools or conventions to celebrate the achievements of women like Jane Addams, Sojourner Truth, and Clara Barton. Along with an impressive assortment of original documents, photographs, and posters, exhibits include Helen Keller Christmas cards, the recorded voice of Florence Nightingale, and actual hair from Elizabeth Cady Stanton.

Some folks say that the age of highway advertising began in West Virginia when the Bloch Brothers Tobacco Company hired itinerant painters to whet the public appetite for their chewing tobacco. Driving through the Mountain State's smaller roads and byways, you can still see faded signs that read "Treat yourself to the Best, Chew Mail Pouch."

A spiritual Disneyland, a United States Taj Mahal, an answer to what those folks have been doing with the money they collect in airports — Prabhupada's Palace of Gold near Wheeling is a bit of all three. Built by devotees of the Hare Krishna movement, the palace advertises itself as being built entirely by untrained hands, individuals who read self-help books with an eye toward God and the glory of their Swami. Gardens, stained glass windows, marble floors, and countless forms of gold welcome visitors. While you're in the neighborhood, cruise north to Chester to visit the World's Largest Teapot. A former Hire's Root Beer hogshead barrel, the addition of a spout, handle, and lid resulted in a highway attraction worth the drive. The Chester Teapot stands fourteen feet tall.

Before you leave, take a moment to pay tribute to Anna Jarvis, for whom Mother's Day was the work of a lifetime. Seeking to honor the spirit of motherhood — particularly her own mother, who envisioned a Mother's Day that would help heal the scars of the Civil War — Jarvis convinced a Methodist minister to hold a Mother's Day service in the town of Grafton. Jarvis imagined this special service as a remembrance for the mothers who decorated the graves of Civil War soldiers regardless of the side for which they fought. Afterward, she commenced a lifelong lobbying effort that resulted in the creation of a national holiday. Today, the site of that Grafton service serves as the International Mother's Day Shrine.

Modern Highways Follow Indian and Pioneer Trails.

W. VA 1863

VISIT WEST VIRGINIA SCENIC CROSSROADS
WEST VIRGINIA PUBLICITY COMMISSION

Wisconsin is sometimes called "America's Dairyland" — and for good reason. You'll find over 350 varieties of cheese; over two billion pounds of the stuff are produced per year. And not just your basic single slice, either. There is something inspiring about big cheese. Not the extra large family size available at the neighborhood grocery store, not the huge Gouda wheel at the company picnic, but a genuinely huge cheese. Even better, imagine the thrill of fake cheese, resplendent in replicated glory, a memory of the real thing said to weigh nearly eighteen tons. The good people of Neillsville are blessed as the home of the World's Biggest Artificial Cheese and Talking Cow, a commemoration of the Colby colossus and talking bovine which

amused (or slightly frightened) visitors to the Wisconsin exhibit at the 1964-65 World's Fair.

Head southeast toward Wisconsin Dells, a family-oriented collection of tourist traps that include the American UFO and Sci-Fi Museum, Circus World Museum, Dells Army Ducks, Dungeon of Horrors, Mass Panic, Storybook Gardens, Tommy Bartlett's Robot World, and more miniature golf courses than you can shake a putter at. Wisconsin Dells represents an epi-

RELAX IN WISCONSIN
Where friends and nature meet.
Write for DESCRIPTIVE LITERATURE
WISCONSIN CONSERVATION DEPT.
STATE CAPITOL
MADISON, WISCONSIN

center of tourist traps, a Mecca of post-cards, and a truly classic example of road-side history.

Pass through Madison, a pleasant enough town as state capitals go, and you make a choice. If you turn west toward Iowa, drop by the Cave of the Mounds, which features rock formations whose spooky similarities to creatures and objects depend just a little bit on lighting and perspective. When exiting Wisconsin's southwestern corner, you'll surely fall into the magnetic field of the "House on the Rock" attraction in Spring Green. Literally named, the house was built in the 1940s by a fellow named Alex Jordan who thought it would be pretty cool to spend his weekends atop a sixty-foot outcropping of sandstone. Pretty soon, local folks came by and asked to take a peek inside. Like any red-blooded entrepreneur, Jordan charged fifty cents for visitors to tour his ramshackle structure. Today, folks drop about twenty bucks to tour an entire complex of amusements at "House on the Rock" — now a mutated mishmash of creepy carousels, eerie Victorian town-scapes, fiberglass sea creatures, and a glass-covered walkway stretching 218 feet over a canopy of trees. Jordan passed on in 1989, but his house continues to expand, the tours continue to lengthen, and the price continues to rise.

If heading east, set your sights on the International Clown Hall of Fame. Dedicated to an art form that continues to amuse and sometimes unnerve, the site celebrates historically significant entertainers such as Red Skelton, Steve "TJ Tatters" Smith, and Willard Scott, who, before his tenure as a *Today Show* personality, served as both Ronald McDonald and Bozo the Clown. The folks at the International Clown Hall of Fame even provide visitors a chance to dress up as clowns and practice time-tested techniques. The food and entertainment may be cheesy, but folks in Wisconsin seem to like it that way.

SECTION OF TENTS IN HORSE-SHOE ROW, COLLEGE CAMP, WISCONSIN - ON LAKE GENEVA   89243

Wyoming has two nicknames. As the Cowboy State, Wyoming recalls its bronco-busting past in which tough and independent men rode the trail. As the Equality State, Wyoming recalls its ambitious spirit that led to the first law in the United States authorizing women's suffrage. Men and women braving the elements and charting their own paths have always found a home in Wyoming.

Of course, extraterrestrial visitors have dropped by as well. Driving west along Interstate 90, exit at Moorcroft and keep an eye peeled for the horizon. Before you know it, a flattened mountain rises out of the ground. Teddy Roosevelt dedicated Devils Tower National Monument in 1906. The strange-looking mountain is the result of a battle between earth, wind, fire, and water. The tower, an 865-foot high volcano core, has been eroded over millions of years by the Belle Fourche River and weathering. Devils Tower served as the backdrop for the 1977 hit film *Close Encounters of the Third Kind.* No trip to northeastern Wyoming is complete without watching *Close Encounters* projected the outside wall of a KOA kampground with the dark tower looming behind.

Heading south along Interstate 25, you're bound to encounter tales of the jackalope, the mythical rabbit with the horns of an antelope. In 1939 a Douglas taxidermist named Doug Herrick "discovered" the beast, known for its carnivore appetites and occasional midnight singing. When visiting the small town, you'll be asked, "Remember the killer rabbits in the movie, *Monty Python and the Holy Grail?* Those were juvenile jackalopes." Douglas prides itself as the home of the jackalope and even

One of Yellowstone National Park's beloved attractions, Old Faithful, erupts less dependably than you might imagine. Every 35 to 120 minutes, the geyser shoots water upward to a height of 184 feet. It's not the biggest, nor the most dependable geyser in the park, but folks from around the world journey to encounter Old Faithful's powerful bursts of water and steam.

hosts summer Jackalope Days with three-legged races, dancing, and plenty of stories about the mysterious creature. Don't forget to visit Jackalope Square to see an eight-foot-tall sculpture of the town's mascot and moneymaker.

Make your way southwest to Rawlins along Interstate 80 and visit one of the few prison museums where you can get strapped down and photographed in a gas chamber where five folks met their earthly justice. This grisly exhibit is merely one highlight of the gruesomely upbeat Wyoming Frontier Prison Museum, on the site of a prison that opened in 1901 and closed eight decades later. Chatty docents delight in telling the tales of tunnel diggers who might have escaped if not for hitting the gas line, and the lifer who was paroled after forty years but asked to be let back in. The better-than-average gift shop includes prison cookbooks, memoirs, and a text on female inmates entitled *Petticoat Prisoners.*

Before you leave, shoot northwest, away from the interstate, and visit the "home of Buffalo Bill." Even though Buffalo Bill was born in Iowa and buried in Colorado, the folks in Cody, Wyoming, proudly claim the Medal of Honor Winner, dime novel hero, Pony Express rider, army scout, Indian hunter, and entertainer as their own. The Buffalo Bill Historical Center

features museums dedicated to the Wyoming ecosystem, the Plains Indians, firearms, and western art. The center's showcase, the Buffalo Bill Museum, provides insight into Buffalo Bill's various Wild West Shows, which included Annie Oakley, Buck Taylor, and even Chief Sitting Bull. For a growing number of turn-of-the-century Americans for whom the West was merely a figure of speech, Buffalo Bill personified the region, its people, and its significance throughout his long and illustrious life.

CREDITS

Alabama Greetings from Alabama - Colourpicture Publications • Boll Weevil Monument - Courtesy of Cooperative Extension System Records, Special Collections & Archives, Auburn University Libraries. • Cullman's Ave Maria Grotto - Courtesy of Ave Maria Grotto. • St. Francis Hotel Courts - Courtesy of Curt Teich Postcard Archives. **Alaska** Greetings from Alaska - Courtesy of Curt Teich Postcard Archives. • The Alaska Highway - C. P. Johnston Company • See Alaska - America's Last Frontier - Author's collection • Santa Clause House - Courtesy of House of Santa Claus. **Arizona** Greetings from Arizona - Tichnor Quality Views • City Cafe and Texaco Station - Courtesy of Curt Teich Postcard Archives and Richard Musante • The Black Cat Cafe - Courtesy of Curt Teich Postcard Archives and Richard Musante • "Tombstone, too tough to die" - Courtesy of Curt Teich Postcard Archives • Sun-Ray Motel - Courtesy of Curt Teich Postcard Archives. **Arkansas** Greetings from Arkansas - Inter City Press • Jordan's Cottages - MWM Color-Litho • "Buy something today" - Author's collection • Tiny Town - Courtesy of Moshinskie family. **California** Greetings from California - Tichnor Quality Views • Motel Inn - Elmo M. Sellers • Bay View Auto Court - Courtesy of Curt Teich Postcard Archives • Route 66 premium table grapes - Author's collection • Aloha Club - Author's collection. **Colorado** Greetings from Colorado - Tichnor Quality Views • Parkview Motel - Nationwide Post Card Co. • State Line Tourist Trap - Baxtone • Idlewild Motel - Courtesy of Curt Teich Postcard Archives. **Connecticut** Greetings from Connecticut - Courtesy of Curt Teich Postcard Archives. • Howard Johnson's Restaurant - Tichnor Quality Views • Going at full speed, Crescent Beach, Conn. - Author's collection • Connecting bridge at Langdon Islands, Norwalk, Conn. - Author's collection. **Delaware** Greetings from Delaware - Tichnor Quality Views • Stuckey's Pecan Shoppe - Baxtone • New Castle Motel - Mellinger Studios. **Florida** Greetings from Florida - Courtesy of Curt Teich Postcard Archives • Moses Tabernacle in the Wilderness - Courtesy of Curt Teich Postcard Archives • Wigwam Village - Courtesy of Curt Teich Postcard Archives • St. Petersburg Recreation Pier - Courtesy of Curt Teich Postcard Archives • Spook Hill - Courtesy of Curt Teich Postcard Archives. **Georgia** Greetings from Georgia – Asheville post card Co. • The Oaks Tourist Court - Colourpicture • Merry El Motel - Drewcolor • Gary's Motel - Tichnor Quality Views. **Hawaii** Greetings from Hawaii – Mike Roberts Productions • Aloha from Hawaii - Author's Collection. • Hula girl - Author's collection. Don the Beachcomber - Author's collection.

Idaho Greetings from Idaho – John W. Graham & Co. • Bidwell's Auto Court - Colourpicture • Idaho Motel Guide - Idaho Motel Association • Sun Valley Idaho - Author's Collection. **Illinois** Greetings from Illinois – Courtesy of Curt Teich Postcard Archives • The Blackhawk Indian room - Courtesy of Curt Teich Postcard Archives • World's Largest Catsup Bottle - Courtesy of World's Largest Catsup Bottle International Fan Club • Spend at least one day in Aurora Illinois. **Indiana** Greetings from Indiana - Courtesy of Curt Teich Postcard Archives • Beauty Rest Tourist Cabins - MWM Color-Litho. • Buckley's Restaurant - Nationwide Post Card Co. • Colonial Modern Cabins - Picto-Cards, Kaiser & Blair. **Iowa** Greetings from Iowa - Courtesy of Curt Teich Postcard Archives • Party Rooms - Author's Collection • Hoover patch - Herbert Hoover Library and Museum. **Kansas** Greetings from Kansas - Courtesy of Curt Teich Postcard Archives • World's Largest Hand Dug Well - Dexter Press. • Never had such a time in my life in Fort Scott, Kan. - Author's Collection. **Kentucky** Greetings from Kentucky - Courtesy of Curt Teich Postcard Archives • Cave City Wigwam Village pennant - Author's Collection • Dutch Mill Village - Courtesy of Curt Teich Postcard Archives • Sanders Courts - E. B. Thomas • G. W. Shoffner Tourist Home - Beals Co. **Louisiana** Greetings from Louisiana - Courtesy of Curt Teich Postcard Archives • Paradise Tourist Court - Skinner & Kennedy Co. • Court of Two Sisters - Author's Collection • Pretty Acres Motel and Country Club - Lion Match Co. **Maine** Greetings from Maine - Courtesy of Curt Teich Postcard Archives • Bay and Camping Field - Underwood Motor Camp • International Signpost - Illustrating Co • Maine Vacationland - Author's Collection. **Maryland** Greetings from Maryland - Del Mar news agency • Thompson's Restaurant - Universal Match Corp. • Old Toll Gate on National Highway Between Cumberland and Frostburg - Marken & Bielfeld, Inc. • The Washington Mayflower Restaurant - Courtesy of Curt Teich Postcard Archives. **Massachusetts** Greetings from Massachusetts – Courtesy of C.T. & Co. • Laconia Restaurant - Ohio Match Company • Mapparium - Tichnor Quality Views • Berkshire Hills - Tichnor Quality Views. **Michigan** Greetings from Michigan - C.T. & co. • Elms Motel - Courtesy of Curt Teich Postcard Archives • Lake Breeze Cabin Court - Author's Collection • Vacation in Michigan - Author's Collection. **Minnesota** Greetings from Minnesota - Courtesy of Curt Teich Postcard Archives • Arrowhead Cafeteria - Ohio Match Company • World's Largest Muskie Drive-in - Northern Minnesota Novelties • Greyhound Origin Center - Courtesy of

Greyhound Origin Center. **Mississippi** Greetings from Mississippi - Courtesy of Curt Teich Postcard Archives • Mid-South Motel - Universal Match Corp. • Alamo Plaza Hotel Courts - Colourpicture • Friendship House - Match Corp of America. **Missouri** Greetings from Missouri - Courtesy of Curt Teich Postcard Archives • Coral Court - Tichnor Quality Views • Siesta Motel - Ad-craft Line, Inc. • Moonlight Motel - Universal Match Corp. **Montana** Greetings from Montana - Courtesy of Curt Teich Postcard Archives • Fred & Millie's Cafe - Lauretta Studio • Mile-Hi Motel - Tichnor Quality Views • Siesta Motel - Lynx Products. **Nebraska** Greetings from Nebraska - Courtesy of E.C. Kropp Co. • Park Motel - Courtesy of Curt Teich Postcard Archives • Omaha Greyhound Union Bus Depot - Quality Views • Main Street of America - Colourpicture. **Nevada** Greetings from Nevada - Courtesy of Tichnor Bros.• Visit Reno on the way - Author's Collection • Have fun in the sun - Author's Collection • Two stiffs selling gas - Courtesy of Curt Teich Postcard Archives. **New Hampshire** Greetings from New Hampshire - Courtesy of Tichnor Bros • English Village East - Courtesy of Curt Teich Postcard Archives • Story Town - Mike Roberts • Drive in today - Author's Collection. **New Jersey** Greetings from New Jersey - Courtesy of Curt Teich Postcard Archives • Atlantic City - Author's Collection • Elephant Hotel - E. C. Kropp Co. **New Mexico** Greetings from New Mexico - Courtesy of Curt Teich Postcard Archives • New Mexico Standard Stations road map - Author's Collection • New Mexico U.S. Highway 66 - Courtesy of Richard Musante • Tewa Lodge - Courtesy of Curt Teich Postcard Archives. **New York** Greetings from New York - Courtesy of C.T. & Co. • Mike's Ship-A-Hoy Yacht Bar - Harry H. Baumann • Pine Ridge Motel - Dorothy Mae Gift Service • The Bird in Hand - Colourpicture. **North Carolina** Greetings from North Carolina - Courtesy of Asheville • Teddy Bear Motel - Universal Match Corp. • Howdy Maggie sez you are now entering Mattie Valley - E. D. DePew • White House Restaurant - Mellinger Studios. **North Dakota** Greetings from North Dakota - Courtesy of Curt Teich Postcard Archives • Mid West Motel - Tichnor Quality Views • Geographical Center of North America - Tichnor Quality Views • Welcome to North Dakota - Saks News, Inc. **Ohio** Greetings from Ohio - Courtesy of Curt Teich Postcard Archives • Parkway Restaurant - Courtesy of Curt Teich Postcard Archives • Kahiki mug - Author's Collection • Amity Hotel Courts - Courtesy of Curt Teich Postcard Archives • Tony Packo's Pickles & Peppers - Courtesy of Tony Packo's Cafe. **Oklahoma** Greetings from Oklahoma - Courtesy of Curt Teich Postcard Archives • Glen's Hik'ry Inn - Match Company • Hik'ry Pit Bar-B-Q - Universal Match Corp. • Oklahoma, Everything's goin' OKAY - Author's Collection. **Oregon** Greetings from Oregon - Courtesy of C.T. & Co. • Come to Oregon - Author's Collection • Stashe's Hollywood Motel - Colourpicture • Rose Manor 99E. Autel - Author's Collection. **Pennsylvania** Greetings from Pennsylvania - Courtesy of Curt Teich Postcard Archives • Apple Valley Village - Pocono Scenicards • Plaster model of Independence Hall - Author's Collection • Milford Diner - Brucelli Adv. Co. **Rhode Island** Greetings from Rhode Island - Berger Bros. • Greetings from Pawtucket - Colourpicture • Monkey Island - Berger Bros. **South Carolina** Greetings from South Carolina - Courtesy of Asheville Postcard Co. • Pocalla Springs Tourist Court - Tichnor Quality Views • Post Exchange Service Station - Courtesy of Curt Teich Postcard Archives • South of the Border - Author's Collection. **South Dakota** Greetings from South Dakota - Courtesy of E.C. Kropp Co. • Wall Drug pennant - Author's Collection • Sky Way Cafe - Tichnor Quality Views • Crystal Cave - Author's Collection • The World's Only Corn Palace - Courtesy of Curt Teich Postcard Archives. **Tennessee** Greetings from Tennessee - Courtesy of Asheville Postcard Co. • Alhambra Courts - Tichnor Quality Views • Glass House - W. M. Cline Co. • Holiday Inn - Courtesy of Curt Teich Postcard Archives. **Texas** Greetings from Texas - Courtesy of Dallas Post • Crockett Court - Courtesy of Curt Teich Postcard Archives • San Antonio - Author's Collection • U-Drop-Inn - Diamond Match Co. **Utah** Greetings from Utah - Courtesy of Curt Teich Postcard Archives • See America First - Colourpicture • Utah Covered Wagon Days - Author's Collection • Dinosaur Motel - L. C. Thorne. **Vermont** Greetings from Vermont - Tichnor Quality Views • Home Town College Club button - Author's Collection • Rates of Toll (Peru, Vermont) - Forward's Color Productions, Inc. **Virginia** Greetings from Virginia - Courtesy of Asheville Postcard Co. • The Old Dominion State - Author's Collection • Traveler's Drive In Restaurant - Universal Match Corp. • Moore's Brick Cottages - Match Corp. of America. **Washington** Greetings from Washington - C.P. Johnston Co. • Washington poster stamp - Author's Collection • The Ranch - The Ohio Match Co. • Our way home - Ellis Post Card Co. **West Virginia** Greetings from West Virginia - Colourpicture • West Virginia, the Mountain State - Author's Collection • Visit West Virginia - Author's Collection. **Wisconsin** Greetings from Wisconsin - Courtesy of Curt Teich Postcard Archives • Relax in Wisconsin - Author's Collection • College Camp - C. R. Childs Co. • Cave of the Mounds - Courtesy of Curt Teich Postcard Archives. **Wyoming** Greetings from Wyoming - Courtesy of Curt Teich Postcard Archives • Lusk - Author's Collection • Jackalope - Petley Studios • Greetings from Old Wyoming - Sanborn Souvenir, Co.

Andrew Wood (Ph.D., 1998, Ohio University) teaches in the communication studies department at San José State University and has co-authored another book entitled *Online Communication: Linking Technology, Identity, and Culture*. A noted website designer, scholar, and public speaker, Dr. Wood's creative work has been celebrated in media outlets including *CNN*, *USA Today*, the *Wall Street Journal*, *Atlantic Monthly*, and National Public Radio's *Morning Edition*. He is married to the former Jenny Boyar. Together, they maintain an award-winning website exploring roadside architecture, called Motel Americana.